ISSUES THAT CONCERN YOU

Student Loans and the Cost of College

Paula Johanson, *Book Editor*

GREENHAVEN
PUBLISHING

Published in 2018 by Greenhaven Publishing, LLC
353 3rd Avenue, Suite 255, New York, NY 10010

First Edition

Copyright © 2018 by Greenhaven Publishing, LLC

First Edition

Articles in Greenhaven Publishing anthologies are often edited for length to meet page requirements. In addition, original titles of these works are changed to clearly present the main thesis and to explicitly indicate the author's opinion. Every effort is made to ensure that Greenhaven Publishing accurately reflects the original intent of the authors. Every effort has been made to trace the owners of the copyrighted material.

Cataloging-in-Publication Data

Names: Johanson, Paula, editor.
Title: Student loans and the cost of college / edited by Paula Johanson.
Description: New York : Greenhaven Publishing, 2018. I Series: Issues that concern you I Includes bibliographical references and index. I Audience: Grades 9-12.
Identifiers: LCCN ISBN 9781534502215 (library bound) I ISBN 9781534502826 (pbk.)
Subjects: LCSH: Student loans--United States--Juvenile literature. I Student loans--Government policy--United States--Juvenile literature. I College costs--United States--Juvenile literature. I Student aid--United States--Juvenile literature.
Classification: LCC LB2340.2 S846 2018 I DDC 371.2/240973--dc23

Manufactured in the United States of America

Website: http://greenhavenpublishing.com

CONTENTS

Young people are told that education is the way to get a good career. In the United States, many employers require applicants to have earned college degrees. But a post-secondary education can be very expensive.

The overwhelming expense in regard to college education is tuition fees. While most or all of the cost of operating a school of higher learning is borne by financial supporters of the school (and by the government if it is a public institution), a portion of the cost is paid in fees charged to students. The tuition fees students pay cover 10% to 20% of the cost of operating a school.

Why charge tuition fees at all? It's a choice. Until recently, Britain (like many European Union countries) gave maintenance grants to post-secondary students to cover tuition fees. The former education minister responsible for changing those grants to loans regrets the move and has spoken out in favor of scrapping tuition fees entirely. In the United States, the states of Tennessee and Oregon, as well as the city of San Francisco, have made community colleges tuition-free for all their residents. Income is not a factor. As of 2017, New York State has made four-year public colleges tuition-free for residents with a family income under $100,000 per year, rising by 2019 to $125,000.

"Universities provide public—not private—goods," Christopher Newfield pointed out in the *Guardian*. "If the social benefits outweigh the financial, it's only fair we charge students accordingly. Free university is affordable, and the benefits to the whole society are far greater than the cost." Communities are strengthened when everyone is taught to read and write; the same is true when students are trained as nurses, or plumbers, or teachers. The benefit to society from the work people do, and the taxes they pay, far exceeds the costs of operating colleges or supporting students. Newfield spoke for the belief that it's a mistake "when a government mistreats a public good as a private good, applies market rules where they don't belong, and makes higher education more expensive and unequal while lowering its social value."

When governments issue loans instead of grants to students, the subsidy is going to the loan collection agencies instead of students.

Around 2010, just under half of American post-secondary students took out a student loan. These days, close to 60 percent of students take out a student loan in order to afford tuition, books, and living expenses. As M. Gleeson noted in a 2016 master's essay for Johns Hopkins University, "The rise in student loans of the past decade is staggering. From 2004 to 2012, the pool of student loan borrowers grew 69 percent, from 23 million borrowers to 39 million borrowers. At the same time the amount that the average borrower had in loans skyrocketed by 70 percent, from $15,000 to $25,000." Gleeson goes on to add, "The amount of debt that is being accumulated is 'considerably larger than amounts incurred by past cohorts,' and the effect of this rising debt is affecting America's younger student loan borrowers." A person's ability to save for retirement, or to become a homeowner, is severely limited while paying back student loans.

To many people, it seems reasonable for a student to take on a moderate debt that can be paid off in five years or less; this debt seems particularly reasonable to credit or collections agencies. But when many students leave school with not $5,000 or $10,000 debt but a crushing burden of debt load more like a mortgage, many aspects of the economy suffer. People who pay a big chunk of their paychecks towards their student loan debt for ten years or twenty years have no budget for planning major purchases like homes, appliances, or vehicles. They purchase fewer clothes and recreational items, too.

While student financial aid in the United States is administered the same way for every citizen, in practice student loan debt can be more of a hardship for people from marginalized groups. The impact of student loan debt is felt differently by different groups of people, instead of being the same for every American student who takes out a loan. Among students of color, for example, a higher percentage will take out a student loan than students who are of European descent. "Under the invisibility of color blindness," writes Pamela Brown in the *South Atlantic Quarterly*, "a predatory debt system was advanced that stripped African Americans of all economic gains subsequent to civil rights and that spread throughout the rest of the economy, impacting generations to come." Though laws ensure that students of color can enroll in college or university and apply for financial aid, employment opportunities after school are not equal for all people, and employment security is not consistent. As well, repayment or interest relief rules don't always acknowledge that people with economic challenges or family responsibilities might need to attend school part-time or take a semester off.

For many people, there are barriers to attending college. Accommodations can make learning at university or community college possible for a person with a disability, or someone who has not had any encouragement or experience while in school, or students whose families are unable to support them financially. It's odd, but there are people who don't think these accommodations—or student financial aid, or any higher education—are fair. Some people "will feel slighted, even cheated, when they believe someone else is getting something extra without merit. And who can blame them? The structure of higher education today makes everyone feel cheated," writes Katie Rose Guest Pryal in *Chronicle Vitae*. "But that's not how ... accommodations work," she noted. "Accommodations are not a zero-sum game. Accessibility—the word I prefer to use—doesn't mean a disabled person is getting more. It means that our shared environment has become one that is welcoming to all people." Because education benefits society, it's good for society to make education available for everyone who can benefit.

The debates surrounding affordability and access to higher education are explored in *Issues That Concern You: Student Loans and the Cost of College*. This is a topic many students find directly applicable to their own lives. After reading this resource, they will come away with enough information from all sides to help them make their own conclusions.

ONE

Funding Higher Education Is a Balancing Act

Larry Gordon

In the following viewpoint, Larry Gordon spotlights the difficulties inherent in making higher education affordable and accessible. The author reports on the 2017-18 budget for higher education in California, in which Governor Jerry Brown has both good news and bad news for students. Although some programs have been given an increase in funding, it will not be enough to avoid tuition fee increases and cuts to scholarship funding. The author shows that to balance a budget, improvements for some usually come at the expense of others. Before writing for EdSource, Gordon wrote about higher education for the *Los Angeles Times*. In 2014, he won an award for education reporting from the California Newspaper Publishers Association.

Gov. Jerry Brown's 2017-18 budget proposals for higher education continue his campaign for more efficiency and access at California's public college and universities, funding ongoing programs to make it easier to transfer from community colleges, improve graduation rates and shorten time to degrees. But Brown triggered some controversy by advocating cuts in aid to middle class students and supporting tuition increases at the University of California and the California State University systems.

"Brown Proposes More Higher Ed Funding, but Phasing Out Middle Class Scholarships," by Larry Gordon, EdSource, January 10, 2017. Reprinted by permission.

At the University of California system, accessibility for some students comes at the expense of others.

If UC and CSU continue efforts to widen access and lower costs, Brown said he would not oppose the first tuition hikes in six years at those two university systems, describing such increases as "probably needed." He wants to keep community college fees frozen at $46 a credit, among the lowest in the nation, in what his budget document said was "a clear signal that the colleges will remain an accessible pathway to postsecondary education."

Brown also wants to allocate $150 million from Prop. 98 funds for grants to community colleges to develop what his budget summary calls "guided pathway" programs. The funds could be used for activities

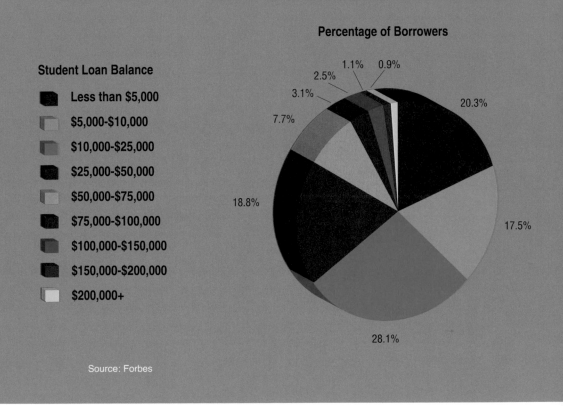

Student loan balance among US borrowers, 2015

Percentage of Borrowers

Student Loan Balance

- Less than $5,000
- $5,000-$10,000
- $10,000-$25,000
- $25,000-$50,000
- $50,000-$75,000
- $75,000-$100,000
- $100,000-$150,000
- $150,000-$200,000
- $200,000+

1.1%   0.9%
2.5%
3.1%
7.7%
20.3%
18.8%
17.5%
28.1%

Source: Forbes

such as designing "academic roadmaps and transfer pathways that explicitly detail courses students must take to complete a credential or degree on time." The goals of the pathway programs would be, among other things, to raise college completion rates, reduce the time it takes to earn a degree and reduce students' debt loads.

In general, higher education officials had a positive reaction to Brown's budget plan. Eloy Ortiz Oakley, chancellor of California Community Colleges, said in a statement that Brown's funding proposal was "good news for community college students" and that extra funding would support programs "aimed at improving student outcomes and fulfilling the promise of a quality college credential for more Californians."

CSU system chancellor Timothy P. White said in a statement that he was "appreciative of the governor's commitment to investing in public higher education" and pledged to keep working on improving graduation rates. A UC statement thanked the governor for the increases and said his budget would help "maintain access, affordability and quality for our students."

The Middle Class Loses Out

However, some middle class students at UC and CSU may be the main losers in Brown's plans unveiled Tuesday. The governor wants to phase out the three-year-old program that provided state-funded financial aid for 46,000 middle class students at California's public universities this year. Critics said his proposal would hurt the chances of other students to attend the universities or put them more in debt. Some legislative leaders said they would fight to preserve the aid.

Brown proposed that the UC and CSU students who receive the Middle Class Scholarship grants this year can continue to do so through 2020-21, but that no new students would be added. Begun in 2014-15, the grants were aimed at easing the tuition burden of families with annual incomes generally between $80,000 and $150,000. Depending on school and income, those grants could be as much as $3,688 this year for a UC student, according to the California Student Aid Commission, which administers the grants.

In the past, opponents of the middle class aid sought to eliminate the grants, saying they drained money from lower income students. On Tuesday, Michael Cohen, Brown's director of the Department of Finance, told reporters that the phaseout was a "difficult choice" but, given worries about a possible state deficit, the move was aimed at preserving the larger Cal Grant program for lower income students. During the next four years, the plan would save about $116 million, the budget estimated. About 356,000 students receive the regular Cal Grants, which range from $1,670 a year at community colleges to about $12,200 at UC.

Lupita Cortez Alcalá, executive director of the California Student Aid Commission, said she was "deeply disappointed" by the governor's plan regarding middle class aid. "This is not the time to backpedal from our commitment to California students," she told EdSource. Without those grants, some students may feel they are "unable to afford attending an institution that they worked really hard to get into," she said. Some legislative leaders, including Assembly Speaker Anthony Rendon, D-Paramount, said they would oppose Brown's idea as well as any tuition hikes.

Rising Tuition Fees

Overall, Brown's budget called for increases in general fund and property tax revenues of $121 million or 1.3 percent for community colleges; and general fund revenue increases of $185 million or 5.3 percent at CSU, and $83 million or 2.5 percent at UC. (UC also would receive an extra $169 million for its pension costs.) While keeping community college fees frozen, Brown told reporters that the proposed university tuition increases are "probably needed." Facing strong student protests, UC is considering an increase of $336 or 2.7 percent for tuition and systemwide fees, and CSU may seek as much as $270 or 5 percent more.

Still, Brown insisted at a press conference that he wanted the universities to lower their cost structures and operate more efficiently to serve more students and help them graduate on time. He warned that budgets could be cut in the future, and that UC and CSU must "build reserves and build resiliency in their programs and not just invoke this amorphous term 'quality' as the justification for more and more spending." He said money should be set aside for "guided pathways" that help community college students with counseling and planning to finish their certificates or degrees and transfer more easily.

Education experts said that much could change by the time the final state budget is approved, depending on such varied factors as tax revenues in California and the policies of the incoming Trump administration. "There are a lot of balls up in the air in the coming months," said Debbie Cochrane, vice president of the

Institute for College Access & Success, an Oakland-based non-profit that seeks to keep college affordable and student debt low.

In general, Cochrane praised Brown for his focus on improving graduation and transfer rates. And she said that she agreed with the governor that if money had to be cut, she too would phase out middle class aid to protect other Cal Grants. "It feels like a no-brainer," she said.

TWO

"College for All" and "Cut Education Budgets" Can't Coexist

Randall Garton

In the following viewpoint, Randall Garton argues that our leaders are talking out of both sides of their mouths when it comes to funding higher education. Politicians attract votes with promises of free tuition, while the reality is that budget cuts are always looming. Today's generation of students is faced with an unenviable decision: Go to college but get saddled with a mountain of debt, or don't go to college and face bleak employment prospects. What is anyone to do? The author suggests that our leaders get together to make creative decisions based in the realm of possibility. Garton is director of research and operations for the Albert Shanker Institute, a nonprofit foundation focusing on public education.

Over the past several years, the mantra of "college for all" has become ubiquitous, with Americans told that a college education is no longer a luxury, but a necessity, for any individual who aspires to a middle-class life in the 21st century economy. And indeed, many studies tend to confirm that persons with a post-secondary education enjoy lower unemployment rates and higher wages over time.

Simultaneously—sometimes in the same articles—we learn that soaring tuition rates have put college out of the reach of

"Higher Education: Soaring Rhetoric, Skyrocketing Costs," by Randall Garton, Albert Shanker Institute, May 4, 2012. Reprinted by permission.

The rising costs of college have made it difficult for parents to fund their children's education.

many, if not most, families. In fact, for the past few decades, college costs have been rising faster than health care costs. In the last year or so, the news is that students who tried to borrow their way around this seemingly intractable problem only dug themselves a deeper hole. Outstanding student college loans have reached—or soon will reach—the $1 trillion mark.

The average student graduates college with a debt burden of nearly $25,000; others, especially those with professional degrees, are buckling under a debt load in the six figures. Since bankruptcy forgiveness does not apply to student debt, even unemployed and underemployed graduates can expect to carry this debt with them for years, perhaps decades, to come. With a slow economy exacerbating the problem, it's no surprise to find that the national student loan default rate for 2009 (the last year for which data are available) was 8.8 percent and rising. At for-profit schools, the rate was 15 percent.

How to Pay?

One alternative, of course, is to rely on parents for help with college. Unfortunately, this has resulted in an emerging crisis for seniors, a growing number of whom go into retirement saddled with the debt they incurred in putting their children through college. Combined with the poor economy, rising tuition rates are forcing parents to rethink what sort of support they can offer their children who plan to attend college. A recent CBS-*New York Times* poll found that 40 percent of parents have been forced to "alter expectations" for the kind of college their children will be able to attend. Others can no longer afford to provide any support.

A second alternative is to adjust our notion of what "college" means. We could urge students to focus on more practical job-related higher education such as that found in community colleges, apprenticeship programs and technical training leading to skill certifications. Those who start with these options can still continue on for the standard four year degree if they want to, but in the meantime they will have the skills they need for a good job. Yet, the economy is taking a toll here as well. Cuts in state government funding have resulted in rapidly escalating costs and severe shortages in seats, just at the time that demand for these programs is greatest.

And, of course, a third alternative is for kids to try to work their way through college, or at least work to supplement the available parental support. I did this. For my working-class parents, there was no choice. I have impressed on my own son the value of combining work and school. It can help our youth start off strong, instilling them with some confidence, a sense of accomplishment, and some financial independence. I believe that. The problem is that it was possible for me because I worked a good union job on

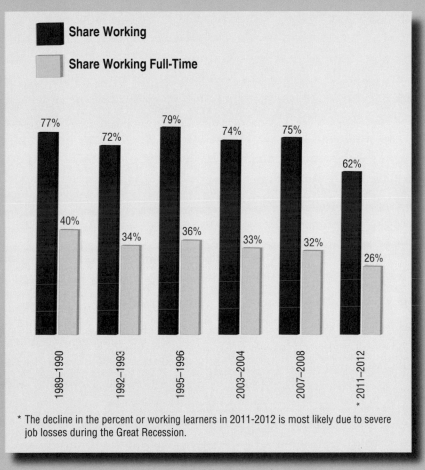

Percentage of US students working while enrolled in Postsecondary institutions, 1989–2011

■ Share Working

☐ Share Working Full-Time

1989–1990	1992–1993	1995–1996	2003–2004	2007–2008	* 2011–2012
77%	72%	79%	74%	75%	62%
40%	34%	36%	33%	32%	26%

* The decline in the percent or working learners in 2011-2012 is most likely due to severe job losses during the Great Recession.

Source: Center on Education and the Workforce, Georgetown University

a factory floor, at a time when those jobs were relatively plentiful and well paid. Where these jobs still exist, they aren't so easy to get, even for experienced adults, let alone for a college kid.

A Realistic Approach Is Needed

So, go to college, and get saddled with crippling debt; don't go, and face a future of dwindling economic opportunity.

Feeling the need to do something, President Obama issued an executive order late in 2011 than would cap student loan repayments at 10 percent of income, rather than the current 15 percent, and forgive all student debt after 20 years. Seems like a nice gesture, but as some critics point out, it doesn't address those skyrocketing costs. And while some reformers urge widespread adoption of distance learning as a cost-cutter, there are many unresolved questions and issues remaining with the distance learning approach, despite some optimism from educators about its future.

So what is to be done? There are no easy answers here. But I would suggest that politicians and policy specialists who trumpet "college for all" out of one side of their mouths and "cut education budgets" out of the other, might want to align their messages with reality. Or just shut up.

THREE

Should University Education Be Free?

Tejvan Pettinger

> In the following viewpoint, Tejvan Pettinger balances the benefits and drawbacks to making university education available to more people. Using the recent changes to UK university system funding as his starting point, the author examines the responsibility a government or society has to educate its citizens. Both societal results and personal results are mentioned. The author pays particular attention to the idea that vocational training is a relevant option for students and for the community at large. A graduate of Oxford University, Pettinger teaches economics and contributes articles to the *Economic Review*.

Summary

Education has positive benefits for the rest of society. If university education is left to market forces, there may be under-provision, and the economy may suffer from lack of skilled graduates. Furthermore, in a free market, higher education would become the preserve of wealthy families who can afford to send their children to university. Therefore there is a strong case for the government providing higher education free at the point of use.

However, others argue the positive externalities of higher education are limited and the prime beneficiaries of a university degree are the graduates who can command a higher paying job. If the external benefits of many degrees are limited, government spending may be misallocated in offering relatively expensive university

In some countries, univeristy education is more affordable or free because it is seen as a benefit to society.

education. Rather than fund 3-4 year university degrees, governments may be able to get a better return from spending money on primary education and vocational training—training which is more relevant to the needs of the economy.

More details

In recent years, the UK government has sought to increase the amount students pay for studying at university. In the UK, the government have phased out grants and introduced top-up fees. With tuition fees and rising living costs, students could end up paying £50,000 for a three-year degree, and leave university with significant debts.

Some argue this is a mistake. Charging for university education will deter students and leave the UK with a shortfall of skilled labour—and arguably this will damage the long-term prospects of the UK economy. Furthermore, charging to study at university will increase inequality of opportunity as students with low-income parents will be more likely to be deterred from going to university.

Arguments for free university education

1. **Positive externalities of higher education.** Generally, university education does offer some external benefits to society. Higher education leads to a more educated and productive workforce. Countries with high rates of university education generally have higher levels of innovation and productivity growth. Therefore, there is a justification for the government subsidising higher education.

2. **Equality.** There is also a powerful argument that university education should be free to ensure equality of opportunity. If students have to pay for university education, this may dissuade them. In theory, students could take out loans or work part-time, but this may be sufficient to discourage students from studying and instead may enter the job market earlier.

3. **Increased specialisation of work.** The global economy has forced countries, such as the UK to specialise in higher tech and higher value-added products and services. The UK's biggest export industries include pharmaceuticals, organic chemicals, optical and surgical instruments, and nuclear technology. Therefore, there is a greater need for skilled graduates who can contribute to these high-tech industries.

4. **Education is a merit good.** One characteristic of a merit good is that people may underestimate the benefits of studying and undervalue higher education. Government provision can encourage people to study.

5. **Non-economic benefits of education.** It is tempting to think of university education in purely monetary terms. But graduates can also gain skills and awareness of civic institutions which offer intangible benefits to society.

Return to society per graduate annually

External Social Benefits	Estimated Value (in dollars)
Democracy	727.34
Human rights	1138.9
Political stability	2312.74
Longer life expectancy	918.88
Less inequality	x
Poverty reduction	1237.26
Lower murder rates	284.72
Lower property crime	1960.71
Lower public welfare/prison costs	216.13
Water, air, forest, wildlife sustainability	2231.2
Increased social capital	y
New ideas and adaptation of R&D	z
Total social non-market benefits	11027.88+x, y, and z

Source: Times Higher Education

Higher Learning, Greater Good: The Private and Social Benefits of Higher Education (2009) Professor McMahon examined the "private non-market benefits" for individuals of having degrees.

This includes better personal health and improved cognitive development in their children, alongside the "social non-market benefits," such as lower spending on prisons and greater political stability.

If you wished to evaluate this point, we could ask—is it university education which causes these civic virtues or is it because university education is dominated by middle classes who are more likely to have better health etc. already?

Arguments against free university education

1. **Opportunity cost**. If we spend billions on free university education there is an opportunity cost of higher taxes or less spending elsewhere. Arguably, there is a greater social benefit from providing vocational training—e.g. so people could become plumbers, electricians etc. There is often a real shortage of these skills in an economy. The UK Commission for skills and education report significant skills shortages in the basic "core generic skills" such as literacy, numeracy and communication skills. These skill shortages are prominent in industries like building, health care, plumbing, social care and construction. Generally, the problem is not a shortage of graduates with art degrees, but lower level vocational skills. Therefore, there is a case for charging students to study at university—allowing higher public spending to tackle more basic skill shortages.

2. **Do we have too many graduates?** In recent decades there has been a rapid rise in the number of graduates. But many graduates are now leaving university to take jobs which don't require a degree. A study by the ONS found that nearly 50% of workers who left university in the past five years are doing jobs which don't require a degree. Therefore, it is a mistake to continue to fund the public expansion of university education because the economy doesn't need more graduates as much as other vocational skills.

3. **Higher quality of education**. The rapid rise in university numbers means that greater pressure is being put on university resources. Since the government is struggling to

increase real spending, there is a danger that university education and research may suffer, causing UK education to lag behind other countries. If universities can charge students, it will help maintain standards, quality of teaching and the reputation of UK universities.

4. **Makes people value education more**. If people have to pay to go to university, you could argue that they would value the education more. If higher education is free, it may encourage students to take an easy three years of relaxation.

5. **Signalling function of higher education**. Arguably, higher education acts as a signal to employers that graduates have greater capacity. As a consequence, people who gain a degree, end up with a relatively higher salary. Therefore, if they financially gain from studying at university, it is perhaps fair they pay part of the cost. This is especially important for middle-class families, who send a higher proportion of people to higher education.

Another issue is whether we need 50% of 18-year-olds to go to university. The increase in student numbers is a significant contributory factor to the increased financial pressures on universities. Rather than encouraging students to automatically go to university (as some schools do), it would be better to encourage more students to take vocational training and avoid three years of academic study. If less went to university, it would mean the cost per student would be relatively lower.

Another issue is how do you charge students for going to university? If students leave university with large debts, this has negative consequences. But, if we finance university education through a graduate tax paid when graduates get a decent income then it may be less of a disincentive.

FOUR

Is It Fair to Charge a Fee for Something That Was Once Free?

Charles M. Gray, Sharon M. Oster, and Charles Weinberg

> In the following viewpoint, Charles M. Gray, Sharon M. Oster, and Charles Weinberg focus on reasons why a nonprofit organization such as a university might choose to charge tuition fees at all. The authors ask heavy-hitting questions about charging fees for education: Isn't the function of a school to teach the community? Why would a government subsidize and support a college that charges its citizens user fees? Will fees encourage users to feel invested, responsible, or harvested? Gray is professor of business economics at the Univeristy of St. Thomas. Oster is professor of management and entrepreneurship at Yale University. Weinberg is professor of marketing and behavioral science at the University of British Columbia.

Why would tax-exempt organizations, which have some freedom from the strictures of the marketplace, willingly subject themselves to satisfying the market for even a part of their budgets? Not merely to get more money, it turns out; but since market failure is a common rationale for why we need nonprofit organizations and why they are free from paying most taxes, nonprofits have to act wisely in setting fees.

"To Fee or Not to Fee? (And Related Questions)," by Charles M. Gray, Sharon M. Oster, and Charles Weinberg, The Nonprofit Quarterly, June 21, 2004. Reprinted by permission.

Fees for service have been charged by nonprofits for years, but research shows that this is becoming an increasingly large proportion of nonprofit budgets. It behooves us, therefore, to know what we are doing when thinking about whether and how to price our services to our constituents. This article describes four of the considerations cited by Oster, Gray, and Weinberg including:

- Whether to charge fees
- How to start or increase fees
- Sliding scales
- Bundling services

These are critical considerations in pricing a program, but they are not the only factors. Readers interested in the practical matters of combining fixed with variable and semi-variable costs as aspects of pricing programs should also refer to the article in the Spring 2003 issue of the *Nonprofit Quarterly* entitled "Is There Enough Overhead in Your Grant?"

To Charge or Not to Charge?

The most powerful argument in favor of charging fees is the discipline of the marketplace—that fees increase accountability to the people receiving services. Getting a third party payer involved (in this case we use the term 'third party' to denote a foundation, healthcare insurer, or government, etc.) in any transaction can divert the accountability so that the organization is more focused on the requirements and satisfaction of the third party payer than on the needs of the recipient. The advantages of relying on revenue from users is that an organization will likely serve users better when its financial/institutional success is directly tied to their satisfaction.

The nonprofit sector's access to third party funding mechanisms means that for some organizations, it may be financially viable to have no charges for services—but this doesn't mean charging is out of the question. As Centro Presente, a Boston-based Central American organization discovered, it can be worth further examination even where the organizational tradition is to

Working part-time can help defray the cost of books and housing, but it's very difficult to fund an entire education this way today.

depend primarily on grants and contracts. When Centro Presente started, many of their constituents were newcomers to the United States and, indeed, had little money to spare. Over time, the organization was faced with cutting back on its core programs because there was less grant money available to support their activities (legal services to immigrants and advocacy on immigration-related issues). The organization began conversations with its constituents to engage them in revisiting the organizational model. These conversations revealed that sufficient numbers had progressed to gainful employment and were more than willing to pay the organization for services, as long as it was providing what they really needed. This change increased revenue and brought the organization closer to the needs of its constituency. Centro Presente still receives grants, but is less dependent on them; and

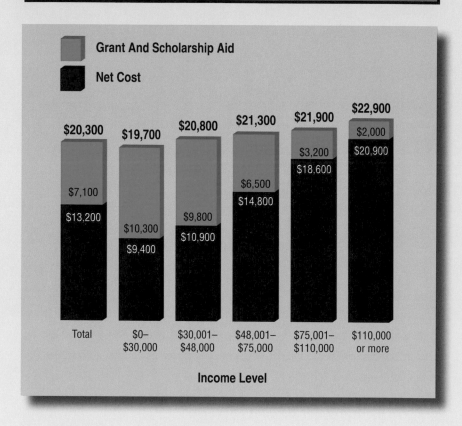

Average total cost, grant and scholarship aid, and net cost of in-state tuition at public four-year institutions, by family income level

Grant And Scholarship Aid

Net Cost

	Total	$0– $30,000	$30,001– $48,000	$48,001– $75,000	$75,001– $110,000	$110,000 or more
Total	$20,300	$19,700	$20,800	$21,300	$21,900	$22,900
Grant And Scholarship Aid	$7,100	$10,300	$9,800	$6,500	$3,200	$2,000
Net Cost	$13,200	$9,400	$10,900	$14,800	$18,600	$20,900

Income Level

Source: National Center for Education Statistics

it has a healthier, more sophisticated, more straightforward—and therefore less encumbered—planning process.

Still, sometimes user fees are not practical given the organization's mission. Many nonprofits, such as Mothers Against Drunk Driving, advocate for things that are socially beneficial but for which there is no direct service to individuals on which fees could be levied. Even though the population as a whole can be said to benefit from MADD's work, the organization has no ability to restrict its benefits to the people willing to pay. In fact, the most appropriate revenue source (and the only one available) is voluntary contributions from people who understand that others, unable to pay, also benefit.

Additionally, as noted in "Pricing in the Nonprofit Sector," "Sometimes charging a fee makes no practical, economic sense. One example of this is when the cost of collecting fees would exceed the revenue raised from such fees." The authors note that this happens most commonly 'when the costs of monitoring usage are very high, for example in a recreational area with no natural fences'."

The authors go on to say, "Numerous studies have suggested that in many circumstances, forcing clients to pay at least some fee, however modest in its revenue-generating properties, creates buy-in for those clients and can be mission-enhancing. In instituting a fee, we have fewer clients, but higher success rates with the clients we do have."

"In an experimental study, Yoken and Berman (1984) demonstrate that before psychotherapy even began, clients who expected not to pay for treatment anticipated gaining significantly less from their sessions than those who were told they would be charged a fee. In a field setting, Kotler and Roberto (1989) reported that patients avoided a newly established free clinic in a South American hospital because, 'they were not convinced of the quality and attention they would receive in the hospital' (p. 175). As a result, the hospital decided to charge a fee and the number of patients increased. However, it should be noted that when clients have a stronger basis for judging product or service quality, the role of price as a cue for high quality is more limited."

"There are also times when charging some fee helps to preserve the dignity of clients served. The Cleveland Jewish Community Center, for example, recently introduced a transportation program for seniors, providing rides for doctor visits, shopping and other activities. Each senior paid '$1 per leg.' Revenue raised in this manner is relatively modest, for there is no real congestion issue, and the service is not intended to change client behavior. The fee clearly does have a role to play by signaling to seniors that they contribute to the program, and that it is not strictly charity.

For populations that are 'newly needy' charging a modest fee may be much preferable to no fee at all."

Fees are a good fit in situations where:

- Collecting fees is practical;
- Access to the service among the intended audience is not cut off through the charging of those fees;
- Accountability to beneficiaries would be significantly augmented;
- The central function or core mission is not subverted. This subversion can occur in several ways, including displacement of primary beneficiaries by more affluent customers, and mission drift to more lucrative pursuits through inattentive managers.

It is wise for managers to think through alternative long-term scenarios and monitor consequences.

How to Transition to Charging Fees

It is one thing to launch a new service with a price attached; it is another and more difficult proposition to attach a price to a service originally provided for no fee. There is a variety of hard-gained experience in the Internet world to support this: "Once people are accustomed to receiving something for free, it is very difficult to get them to pay for it."

Some organizations have found that they can make a gradual transition to charging if they "continue to offer a version of the product free, while offering a preferred option at some price. Arts organizations that begin by offering free concerts will find it easier to introduce pricing if they maintain some free seats (or some free performances). The Kennedy Center coupled a substantial increase in admissions fees with increased attention to free performances. Health clinics that initiate co-pays for service might limit those co-pays for certain essential health services."

The over-riding suggestion in this chapter on making the transition from no-cost to cost-based services is this: It is easiest to institute a price for an already-existing service when there is a significant upgrade or change in that service, the key word being significant. A related caution is that when a new or redeveloped service is initiated, there are frequently startup costs greater than planned. Organizations should budget cautiously for development, evaluation, and fine-tuning of the program, as well as for development costs for new financial controls and the installation of mechanisms to collect and process payments.

Considerations About Sliding Scales

Nonprofits are active users of differential pricing, usually in the form of sliding scales, but they are not particularly scientific in their approaches to it. Theoretically, a sliding scale carries with it the potential for alienating clients who are paying full freight. But for many nonprofits, the advantages to differential pricing are clear: it provides access to those who might otherwise be excluded; it allows for income diversity among program users; and it provides a larger market for the service. Oster, Gray and Weinberg assert that the apparent key to success in establishing and maintaining a sliding-scale fee structure is transparency combined with voluntary participation.

Here are some good examples: "a small preschool program in New Haven charges day care prices on a sliding scale related to voluntary reporting of parental income and supported by an explicit ideology of inclusion. In these cases, there is a kind of voluntary or at least cooperative price discrimination and some attempt to promote buy-in of the principle of differentials. Some museums take an intermediate stance, treating admissions fees as voluntary donations, but listing a 'suggested' fee. For modern day colleges, the picture is rather different. For many in the college world, differential pricing is a tool that improves institutional quality for all students, by allowing colleges to accept a student population without regard to ability to pay. Nevertheless, tuition differences are imposed, not chosen, and the ideological and practical importance of these price differentials, however clear they are to administrators, are not always widely embraced by parents. The result, in some colleges, is a growing resentment and gaming of the system."

"For nonprofits that want to practice differential pricing, the lessons are clear: The more cooperative or voluntary such differentials appear, the less resistant clients will be to them. When differentials are imposed, rather than chosen, the nonprofit has a burden to convince clients of the value of the differentials in terms of product improvements for everyone. Winston and Zimmerman (2000), for example, suggest that colleges remind parents that even those students who pay the full $31,000 tuition are paying only a portion of the true total costs of an education. In this way, the point is made that in organizations supported in part by donative funds and/or endowments, each client is typically subsidized, and it is simply a question of how deep those subsidies are for different people. Again, in the college setting, making the case for the role of diversity of all sorts in improving the college experience for all students is vitally important in reducing resistance to pricing differentials. For organizations like hospitals and arts organizations, with substantial infrastructure or fixed costs, differential pricing may help to expand the audience in ways that lower the overall average production costs."

Notes

1. This article was prepared in collaboration with the publisher and authors of the publication, however, any deviations from the original chapter, intentional or accidental, remain the responsibility of the Nonprofit Quarterly.

2. Sharon M. Oster is the Frederick Wolfe Professor of Entrepreneurship and Management at the Yale School of Management; Charles M. Gray, Ph.D. is a professor of economics at the University of St. Thomas, where he has taught economics and strategy to MBA students in the full-time and evening programs for more than 25 years; Charles B. Weinberg is a professor of marketing at the Sauder School of Business at the University of British Columbia.

3. To order Effective Economic Decision-Making by Nonprofit Organizations, see the Foundation Center Web site: http://fdncenter.org/marketplace/catalog/product_monograph.jhtml?id=prod440002. Other chapters in the book cover topics including: compensation, outsourcing, fundraising costs, investment and expenditure strategies, nonprofit commercial ventures, institutional collaboration, and Internet commerce and fundraising.

4. See "In but not Of the Market: The Special Challenge of Nonprofit-ness," by Ruth McCambridge and Lester Salamon in the Spring 2003 issue of the Nonprofit Quarterly for a further discussion of this topic.

FIVE

When It Comes to Loan Repayment, Quality Matters

Sandra Black, Amy Filipek, Jason Furman, Laura Giuliano, and Ayushi Narayan

> In the following viewpoint, Sandra Black, Amy Filipek, Jason Furman, Laura Giuliano, and Ayushi Narayan argue that the quality of the higher learning institution directly affects the value of the student loan. On average, student loans enable students to gain employment with higher earnings. Borrowers who attend low quality schools face difficulties with repayment, as do those who fail to complete their degree or certification. Black is an Economics professor at University of Texas. Filipek is Staff Economist for the Council of Economic Advisers. Furman is chair of the Council of Economic Advisers. Giuliano is an associate professor of Economics at University of Miami and Senior Economist for the Council of Economic Advisers. Narayan is Research Economist for the Council of Economic Advisers.

Student debt has increased rapidly in the US over the past 20 years and currently totals over $1.3 trillion. A rising number of students are taking out loans, and today, roughly half of students borrow to pay for the tuition and living expenses associated with a college education. This trend has led some to question whether we are facing a student debt "crisis," and a growing body

"Student Loans and College Quality: Effects on Borrowers and the Economy," by Sandra Black, Amy Filipek, Jason Furman, Laura Giuliano, and Ayushi Narayan, VoxEU.org, August 4, 2016. Reprinted by permission.

Students rack up a number of secondary fees aside from tuition costs. There are textbooks and materials, room and board, transportation, and all kinds of miscellaneous expenses to pay for.

of research has assessed the validity of this claim (e.g. Avery and Turner 2012, Looney and Yannelis 2015). A new report by the Council of Economic Advisers (2016) offers a comprehensive perspective on the economic benefits and challenges of student loans. Drawing on current research and new data from the Department of Education, it shows that on average, student loans facilitate very high returns for college graduates in the form of a high earnings premium, and most borrowers are able to make progress paying back their loans. But, borrowers who attend low quality schools or fail to complete their degree face real challenges with repayment. And even students whose lifetime return far exceeds their debt can have trouble with repayment at the start of their careers, when they are starting out and are not reaping the full earnings benefit of their additional education. Addressing these challenges has been a high priority of the Obama Administration, and policies to help students make better enrollment choices, better regulate for profit educational institutions, and make repayment more flexible, particularly through models allowing payments to vary with income, have begun to show results.

The benefits of higher education greatly outweigh the costs, on average

The college earnings premium has grown steadily over the past several decades and reached historical levels in recent years. Compared to high school graduates, bachelor's degree recipients typically earn $500,000 more in present value over their lifetime—well above the roughly $30,000 of debt that borrowers accumulate on average for that degree. With such high returns, higher education is typically a strong investment, and most who borrow are able to repay their debt.

While part of the increase in total student debt is due to the increase in the number of students who enroll in college, there has also been an increase in the typical amount of debt that borrowers accumulate. One explanation for this is increasing college costs, in part due to a decline in state funding for public colleges. However, while published costs have risen sharply over the past couple of decades, a doubling of investments in Pell Grants and tax credits has helped to moderate the impact on the net price that students pay. Indeed, most students accumulate only modest amounts of debt: 59% of borrowers owe less than $20,000 in debt, with the undergraduate borrowers holding an average debt of $17,900 in 2015. Similarly, large-volume debt remains more prevalent among graduate loans.

All this suggests that, on average, the benefits of borrowing to invest in a college education continue to far exceed the costs.

But many students still face debt challenges, especially due to variation in college quality and completion

While the earnings premium is typically very high, the returns students see after they leave school vary significantly. Students who fail to complete a degree or attend a low-quality institution that does not strengthen their labour market prospects can see lower returns (e.g. Hoekstra 2009, Cellini and Turner 2016) and face difficulty in repaying loans.

One important predictor of repayment difficulty is the failure to complete a degree. This relationship is so strong that it leads to a counterintuitive pattern in repayment outcomes: students with the smallest loan balances actually struggle the most with repayment. These students typically have lower balances because they have spent less time in school and are also the least likely to have completed a degree. In fact, the data show that loan size, for the most part, is positively related to the ability to repay. Large-volume debt is far more prevalent among graduate students, who have the higher earnings and thus a lower probability of default.

Similarly, among undergraduate borrowers, those with the largest debt size are more likely to have completed a degree, which decreases the probability of default regardless of debt size. Among those who complete a degree, undergraduate borrowers who graduated with less than $5,000 in debt have similar likelihoods of defaulting as those who graduated with larger amounts of debt. However, fewer than 1 in 6 undergraduate borrowers with only

$5,000 of initial debt completed college, compared to nearly 2 in 3 borrowers with over $20,000 in debt.

Another related correlate of repayment is college sector. In particular, compared to students who attend community colleges or other non-selective schools, students at for-profits institutions tend to have lower earnings but hold larger amounts of debt (Deming et al. 2012, 2013). More rigorous research confirms that for-profit colleges offer lower returns than other sectors (Cellini and Turner 2016, Cellini and Chaudhary 2013). Consistent with this research, data from the Department of Education show that for-profit students face high rates of default—which is especially concerning in light of the high borrowing rate at these schools. Low-income borrowers and those who attend part-time are also more likely to default, in a pattern consistent with the type of schools they attend and their propensity to complete a degree.

While a challenge for some people, the aggregate macroeconomic effects of student debt are limited

Additional college education, even if financed by student debt, is a big net positive for the economy—increasing skills, productivity, earnings and output. Conditional on a certain amount of college education, additional debt can be a small negative for the economy through reduced expenditures such as home purchases—although, to date, it has not had a large macroeconomic effect in part because as student debt has risen other debt has fallen.

The evidence is clear that the rise in student debt differs in important ways from the rise in mortgage debt. Although student debt has risen to be the second largest category of consumer debt, it continues to make up a small share of aggregate income. In 2015, total student loan debt was 9% of aggregate income, up from 3% in 2003. At its peak in 2007, total mortgage debt was 84% of aggregate income, up 25 percentage points in less than five years. Additionally, the private financial system is not exposed to student loan defaults in the way it was to subprime mortgages since the vast majority of student loans are explicitly guaranteed by the US government.

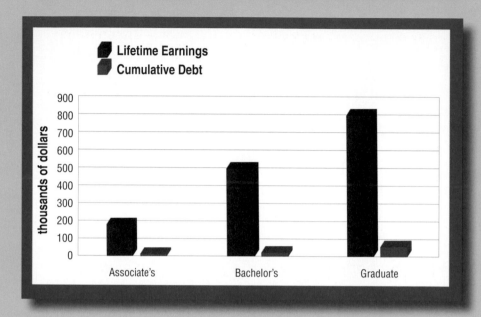

Average monetary value of added lifetime earnings versus average cumulative debt, by degree level

Lifetime Earnings
Cumulative Debt

thousands of dollars

900
800
700
600
500
400
300
200
100
0

Associate's   Bachelor's   Graduate

Source: CPS ASEC 2014 and 2015; NPSAS 2012

Some recent research has found that higher student loan balances—conditional on the same amount of education—can lower homeownership rates. However, these estimates can explain less than a quarter of the decline in homeownership among young households over the last decade and do not incorporate the positive impact of higher education levels. Research that takes into account the positive impact of college highlights that education levels drive home ownership more than debt levels. A study by Mezza et al. (2014) has shown that while early in life those with a college education and no student loan debt are more likely to be homeowners than those with debt, by age 34, their homeownership rates are nearly identical and more than 10 percentage points higher than for those without a college education.

The Obama Administration's policies are also helping

To help more students gain the economic benefits of higher education while minimising the risks of failing to complete a degree and receiving a low-quality education, the Obama Administration has implemented a number of evidence-based policies. To address information barriers about the return to individual colleges, the Administration has improved information about college cost and quality through the new College Scorecard, and it has protected students from low-quality schools through landmark regulations that will cut off federal aid to career college programmes consistently failing accountability standards. Recent improvements to the Free Application for Federal Student Aid (FAFSA) are helping to reduce procedural complexities that can prevent students from applying for aid. And increases in Pell Grants and tax aid have offset much of the rise in college tuitions.

Finally, the Administration has made significant progress toward making debt repayment more manageable by providing borrowers with more flexibility in their repayment options. Data show that the college earnings premium increases substantially over time. Yet the standard repayment plan requires fixed level payments over ten years—imposing constraints that may lead to needless repayment difficulties. The expansion of flexible income driven repayment plans such as the President's Pay as You Earn (PAYE) plan has lifted these constraints for millions of borrowers. These plans better align the timing of loan payments with the timing of earnings benefits by allowing borrowers to make smaller payments early in their careers and to adjust their payments as their earnings grow.

Today, about 5 million borrowers are enrolled in PAYE and other income driven repayment plans, representing a dramatic increase over the past four years. Data presented in CEA's report show that these plans disproportionately help borrowers from lower income families, and those who have struggled to repay their debt. Still, more work remains to increase enrollment in these plans by all those who could benefit from them.

SIX

There Is a Student Debt Crisis

Anne Johnson, Tobin Van Ostern, and Abraham White

In the following viewpoint, Anne Johnson, Tobin Van Ostern, and Abraham White discuss predatory elements in the student loan crisis affecting American students. There is an element of race in the student debt crisis, as more students of color rely on student loans. The student loan reforms passed in 2010 by President Barack Obama shifted some government funding from loan servicers to students. The authors work for the Center for American Progress. Johnson is the Director of Campus Progress. Van Ostern is the Deputy Director of Campus Progress. White is the Communications Associate for Campus Progress.

Higher education is an integral part of the American Dream. But today more and more young people increasingly have to finance their education through student loans.

In the past three decades, the cost of attaining a college degree has increased more than 1,000 percent. Two-thirds of students who earn four-year bachelor's degrees are graduating with an average student loan debt of more than $25,000, and 1 in 10 borrowers now owe more than $54,000 in loans.

African American and Latino students are especially saddled with student debt, with 81 percent of African American students and 67 percent of Latino students who earned bachelor's degrees

The student debt that so many are saddled with affects our entire economy.

leaving school with debt. This compares to 64 percent of white students who graduate with debt. With $864 billion in federal loans and $150 billion in private loans, student debt in America now exceeds $1 trillion.

How Did We Get Here?

Many factors have contributed to the dramatic increase in student debt, including the global economic recession of 2008, which led to a dramatic rise in college enrollment and consequently more students borrowing to pay for school.

One of the major self-inflicted causes is the consistent decline in state funding for higher education, which had helped colleges

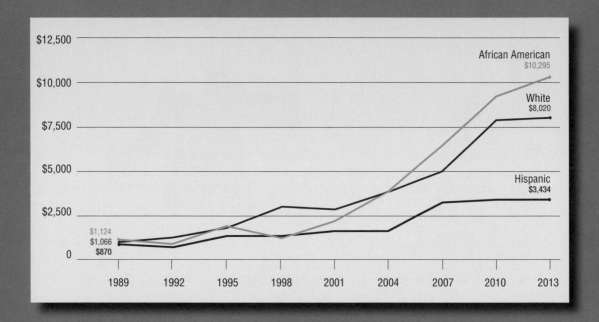

Average family student loan debt by race, 1989–2013

African American	$10,295
White	$8,020
Hispanic	$3,434

$12,500

$10,000

$7,500

$5,000

$2,500

0

$1,124
$1,066
$870

1989 1992 1995 1998 2001 2004 2007 2010 2013

Source: Urban Institute, via Huffington Post

keep tuition affordable. The steadily and rapidly increasing cost of college nationwide prompted a dramatic rise in student borrowing—a natural result as families could no longer rely on scholarships, grants, and personal savings, which cannot keep up with the rapidly increasing tuition costs that have far outpaced the rise in other basic costs like those of health care, gas, and food.

Beyond the job losses and decreased savings, the recession also had a major impact on state colleges and universities directly. One major effect was a drop in colleges and universities' endowment values, which meant that they had fewer dollars to distribute in grants and scholarships to the students who rely on them to pay for school. The recession also led to significant cuts in state higher education funding and consequently a further uptick in tuition.

Another cause has been the rise of the for-profit college sector. Students at non-four-year, for-profit colleges have seen the largest increase in student loan debt among any group of student borrowers. In 2001, 62 percent of freshmen at these schools took out student loans—and just eight years later, that number jumped to 86 percent. These trends are a result of a lack of oversight of private lenders and the marketing practices of these loans by for-profit schools in particular.

These practices include direct marketing to borrowers who are often unaware of all their options, a tactic that has been widely criticized for the part it's played in saddling borrowers with unmanageable levels of debt. Additionally, these schools have made a concerted effort to market to and recruit veterans, even relying on third-party marketing firms who create the illusion that they are part of or endorsed by the federal government—using websites like GIbill.com—and that these for-profit colleges are the only ones accepting Post-9/11 G.I. Bill education benefits. The result is often exhausted benefits and unnecessary student debt.

One of the most troubling segments of student lending, however, is the private student loan sector. Defaulted private loans alone currently total more than $8.1 billion, representing 850,000 individual loans. Because these loans often carry high and variable interest rates, many students can end up paying far more than the cost of tuition.

Private student lending has become so great a concern among students, schools, and higher education advocates that the Consumer Financial Protection Bureau dedicated an entire report to the subject. Over the last decade, the demand for securities backed by these loans led to a dramatic growth in private student lending. From 2005 to 2011 alone, total private student loan debt more than doubled from $55.9 billion to $140.2 billion.

Regardless of which kind of loan students take out (federal or private), all student borrowers face the challenge of repaying their loans—specifically, navigating the bureaucracy involved with the private companies contracted by the original lender (federal and private) to oversee and facilitate repayment. But the problem is more than these loan servicers being unresponsive or unhelpful.

Over the last year 1 million borrowers saw their loans arbitrarily assigned (some only notified after the fact) to a new company, which has resulted in fluctuation of their payments, being put in forbearance, and other inaccuracies in their statements.

A Critical Issue

Major progress was made with the student loan reforms President Barack Obama signed in 2010, which eliminated $60 billion in unnecessary subsidies to private lenders. Those funds were put toward grants for low-income students and the federal government began making fixed, low-interest loans directly to students.

Behind these stark national numbers is the impact these trends are having on students. In fact, the impact often extends beyond the students, burdening their families for decades. This threatens the ability of current and future generations to build successful careers and contribute to the economy, and it affects the ability of previous generations to save for their own future.

Indeed, the overwhelming debt many students face leave them unable to wait for higher-paying jobs and forces them to take lower-paying jobs in order to stop the payments and interest from ballooning. This results in fewer graduates starting their own businesses and negatively impacts the economy. Though many with federal student loans have the option of income-based repayment—a recently expanded program which caps borrowers' required monthly payments at an affordable amount based on income and family size—the majority of borrowers with federal student loans are either unaware or do not understand the program. Additionally, this is not even an option for those with private student loans.

Furthermore, the escalation of college costs has resulted in many students and families barely scraping by, having to turn down admissions to their top-choice schools they couldn't afford, or delaying college altogether. Worse still, some students leave school with debt and no degree.

Despite these issues, higher education remains critical for millions of students and their families. Recent reports from the

Bureau of Labor Statistics now show that college graduates are nearly twice as likely to find work as those with only a high school diploma. The current unemployment rate for those with a college degree—4.1 percent—is about half of the national average. For individuals, it provides a clear path to the middle class, a higher likelihood of gainful employment, and life-long financial and personal benefits. An advanced degree also provides for a skilled workforce that is crucial to rebuilding the American economy.

SEVEN

The Student Loan Crisis Isn't What You Think

Claudio Sanchez

> In the following viewpoint, Claudio Sanchez interviews financial expert Sandy Baum about his book on student loan debt. Baum has some cogent points to make about which students are burdened by this debt, and who defaults. Many people have the perception that college graduates are unable to find good jobs, but Baum disspells that notion. There are other students who incur debt with little potential for paying it off, Baum says, incuding non-traditional students and those attending for-profit universities. Baum has been a senior fellow at the Urban Institute, a think-tank based in Washington, DC. Sanchez works as a journalist on National Public Radio.

There's a new book out about the student loan crisis, or what author Sandy Baum suggests is a "bogus crisis." Baum, a financial aid expert and senior fellow at the Urban Institute, claims it has been manufactured by the media in search of a spicy story and fueled by politicians pushing "debt free college" proposals.

We had a few questions for Baum about the book, *Student Debt: Rhetoric and Realities of Higher Education.*

Roughly 43 million people today hold more than $1.3 trillion in student loan debt. And many are struggling to pay the

Nontraditional students can have difficulty paying off student loans.

money back. But you say Americans have been misled about the seriousness of the problem?

I think what is most important is for people to understand that the common image of the student loan problem really misses the point. People have an image of a recent bachelor's degree recipient who went to college for four years and is now 22-23 years old and is working at Starbucks. Those people are very rare.

People who earn bachelor's degrees, by and large, do fine.

The problem is that we have a lot of people actually borrowing small amounts of money, going to college, not completing [a degree] or completing credentials that don't have labor market value. They tend to be older. They tend to come from disadvantaged, middle-income families and they're struggling. [But] not because they owe a lot of money.

In your book you argue that the student loan crisis has been manufactured to justify loan forgiveness and other schemes. You say proposals like those put forth by Bernie Sanders and Hillary Clinton touting "free college for all" and "debt-free college" are simplistic ... even misguided.

It's not realistic to say we're going to pay people to go to college [for free]. Someone has to pay. We can have everyone pay much higher taxes. But short of that, it's not clear how we would pay.

For the record, you have advised Hillary Clinton's campaign on higher education issues.

Yes. The focus on college affordability, on access to college and removing financial barriers, is very important. [But] how we solve those problems has to be decided in the policy arena rather than in the throes of a political campaign.

You also cite two big trends in your book. First, the surge of older students who've enrolled in college full time, mostly people in their mid to late 20s. Second, you write about the dramatic growth of for-profit schools that require students to borrow more money than they would at public institutions.

It is true that for-profit schools are disproportionately associated with big student debt problems. [But] you have to be careful about painting any sector with a broad brush because there are certainly for-profit schools that serve students well and there are public and nonprofit private schools that don't. That said, a growing proportion of student debt is held by students who went to for-profit institutions. That sector enrolls low-income, older students. It does well getting people short-term certificates. Some pay off, some don't.

You blame the media, though, for inaccurately reporting that the student debt problem is widespread throughout higher

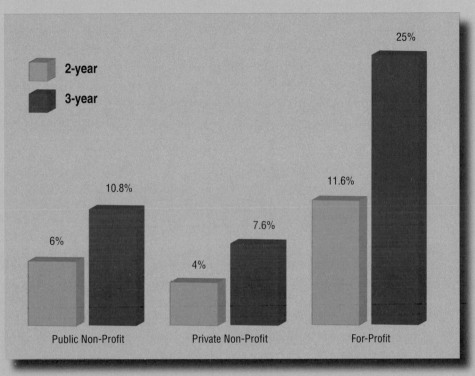

Student loan default rates by education sector

2-year

3-year

Public Non-Profit: 6%, 10.8%

Private Non-Profit: 4%, 7.6%

For-Profit: 11.6%, 25%

Source: US Department of Education

education. **You say your research shows that the actual number of borrowers who are truly struggling is not that big, and that we know exactly which institutions have saddled students with too much debt with little to show for it.**

Exactly. There are some people who borrowed under fraudulent, deceptive situations and their debt should be forgiven. There are people for whom education did not work out through no fault of their own and their debt should be forgiven.

Twenty-four percent of those who left school without a degree, defaulted. So non-completion is a huge problem.

Some schools don't serve students well. Some students aren't prepared to succeed no matter where they go to college.

We just tell everybody: "Go to college. Borrow the money. It will be fine."

We don't give people very much advice and guidance about where ... when to go to college, how to pay for it, what to study.

So if we've exaggerated the seriousness of the student debt problem, should we stop worrying?

I'm not suggesting we shouldn't worry. There's plenty to worry about. [But] we should worry about the single mother of two, going back to school in her late 20s to try to get some training to help her get a job and support her children. We need to worry about supporting her and directing her in a way that will allow her to succeed. We should worry about her student debt. We should worry a lot less about 18-year-olds going off to college and borrowing $20,000, $25,000, for a bachelor's degree.

Finally, in your book you cite some figures that you say get little or no attention because they don't fit the "crisis" narrative:

- A third of college students who earn a four-year degree graduate with no debt at all. Zero.

- A fourth graduate with debt of no more than $20,000.

- Low-income students hold only 11 percent of all outstanding [student] debt.

- Almost half of the $1.3 trillion in student loan debt is held by 25 percent of graduates who are actually making a pretty high income.

You say this is proof that people clearly benefit by borrowing for college because it pays off later.

This is an investment that pays off really well. The median earnings for young bachelor's degree recipients is about $20,000 a year higher than the median earnings for high school graduates.

Student debt is really creating a lot of opportunities for people. People wouldn't be able to go to college otherwise.

EIGHT

Student Loans Are Marred by Corruption

Naomi Spencer

> In the following viewpoint, Naomi Spencer uncovers an alarming amount of corruption regarding student loans. An investigation into student loan companies and college admissions departments by the New York State Attorney General in 2007 led to a web of corruption, deceit, and conflicts of interest at the expense of college students and their families. The trend for increased borrowing through student loans has seen not only rising profits among student aid lenders, but conflicts of interest and shady deals now under state and federal investigation. Spencer was the Socialist Equality Party's candidate in the West Virginia House of Delegates and is the author of the book *Every Decision Yields a Consequence*.

A widening investigation by New York Attorney General Andrew Cuomo's office into dealings between college financial aid administrators and for-profit student loan companies has revealed extensive conflicts of interest, payments, and arrangements benefiting company shareholders at the expense of students and their families.

Last week, investigators found that Matteo Fontana, the Office of Federal Student Aid general manager, a position that makes him responsible for regulating student aid lenders, sold thousands of shares of a student loan company stock in 2003.

At the same time, three senior financial aid officers at three major universities were found to have sold large numbers of shares

"US: Investigation Exposes Extensive Corruption in Student Loan Dealings," by Naomi Spencer, World Socialist Web Site, April 11, 2007. Reprinted by permission.

in the same company, Student Loan Xpress. The actions of these administrators were revealed in an investigation by Higher Ed Watch, part of the government watchdog group New America Foundation. Three other administrators are under investigation by Cuomo for similar relationships with Student Loan Xpress.

"This is like peeling an onion," Cuomo commented to the Associated Press April 10. "It seems to be getting worse the more we uncover. It's more widespread than we originally thought.... More schools and more lenders at the top end."

Cuomo speculated that dozens of other universities would be drawn into the investigation. "No one is even defending the situation anymore," he said. "When we first started, it was 'Oh, this is just a few bad apples.'"

Exploitative and Self-Serving Practices

According to the College Board, university tuition has risen by 35 percent in the last five years. Meanwhile, federal and state grant aid based on financial need has declined. Not surprisingly, as students and their families turned increasingly to private loans, the for-profit student loan industry ballooned into an $85-billion-a-year enterprise.

Private loan companies have worked systematically to develop connections with a layer of elite administrators whose relation to the student population is increasingly exploitative and centered on self-enrichment. According to Cuomo, the owners of Student Loan Xpress developed a deliberate plan to "market to the financial aid offices of schools" in order to increase their share of college lending.

Loan companies cater to administrators at universities by offering financial rewards and incentives for higher loan volume and a place on campus "preferred lender" lists, which students are referred to for their financial needs by aid offices. A loan company that is able to get on such a list will generally receive much more business from students at the school, even though they may not provide the lowest rates.

Many students have turned to private loans, but the for-profit student loan industry is marred by corruption.

Many loan officers attend all-expenses-paid cruises and retreats, and receive complimentary trips, gifts, and bonuses based on the amount of student borrowing each semester.

The three administrators examined in the Higher Ed report were David Charlow, an aid administrator at Columbia University, Lawrence Burt, associate vice president and director of student financial aid at the University of Texas at Austin, and Catherine Thomas, associate dean of admissions and director of financial aid at the University of Southern California.

Charlow sold 7,500 shares in Student Loan Xpress for $72,000 in 2003, and held options on another 2,500 shares. He sold

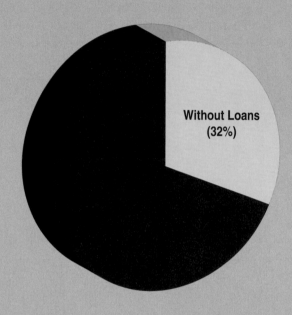

Without Loans (32%)

Source: CNN

additional shares in 2005, bringing his total profit to more than $100,000. According to Higher Ed Watch, Burt sold 1,500 shares at about $10 a share in 2003 and held 500 options on additional shares. Thomas held 1,500 shares.

Charlow, Burt and Thomas all sit on an advisory board for Student Loan Xpress. Higher Ed Watch was unable to determine whether the three had purchased the stock they held or received it as a gift.

However, Higher Ed Watch found that Student Loan Xpress was strongly promoted by Charlow's office. At Columbia University, the company was the largest lender, accounting for 39 percent of the school's total federal loan volume, or $14 million a year. By comparison, the next largest lender, Citibank, provided $5 million in loans to students and their parents last year. Charlow also wrote an endorsement for Student Loan Xpress that appeared on the company's website.

On Monday, financial aid directors at Johns Hopkins University, Widener University and Capella University, an online school based in Minneapolis, Minnesota, were put on paid leave after Cuomo's office found they received tens of thousands of dollars in consulting fees and perks.

The three administrators were suspended after Cuomo's office sent letters to the schools announcing an expansion of its investigation into the dealings.

Ellen Frishberg, student financial services director at John Hopkins University, received $43,000 in consulting fees from Student Loan Xpress and $22,000 in tuition payments for classes she was enrolled in at another school. Frishberg also served on the company's advisory board and wrote an endorsement on its website. According to Cuomo's office, every year for the last four years, more than 40 percent of Johns Hopkins students and their families took out loans through Student Loan Xpress.

Capella University's financial aid director, Timothy Lehmann, was paid $13,000 in consulting fees. At Widener University, the dean of the financial aid office, Walter Cathie, ran a separate company that held conferences on student loans. According to an attorney working at the New York Attorney General's office, Student Loan Xpress paid Cathie's company $80,000 to send representatives to the conferences.

CIT Group, the parent company of Student Loan Xpress, placed three top executives on leave in response to the rapidly expanding investigation.

Student Loan Xpress is not the only company that has been embroiled in the revelations. In March, Cuomo announced that he planned to bring a civil lawsuit against Education Finance Partners of San Francisco for giving what amounted to kickbacks to a number of schools—including St. John's University, Long Island University, Boston University, Clemson University and Baylor University—in exchange for more student loan business.

Earlier this month, without admitting wrongdoing, financial giant Citigroup agreed to pay $2 million to educate students about loans, in response to similar revelations involving the bank's relationship to Syracuse University, New York University, St. John's, Fordham University and the University of Pennsylvania. The universities agreed to pay a total of $3.2 million to student borrowers.

Far-Reaching Conflicts of Interest

Cuomo's investigation last fall also found that at several universities, financial aid call centers were directly but covertly operated by for-profit loan companies in the schools' names—that is, students who thought they were calling the university for financial advice were in fact directed to private loan institutions. The investigation has also examined cases in which loan companies have given universities "opportunity pools" of private, high-interest-rate loan money for students with bad credit in exchange for being named as the exclusive provider of federally managed loans on campus.

The integration of interests extends into the government itself, as indicated by the case of Fontana, the Office of Federal Student Aid general manager who was found to have sold thousands of shares of Student Loan Xpress. He was listed in documents filed with the Securities and Exchange Commission as holding at least 10,500 shares in Education Lending Group, the parent company of Student Loan Xpress at the time. Fontana sold the shares for $10 apiece, collecting more than $100,000.

This shareholding constitutes a conflict of interest with Fontana's 2002 appointment as manager of the National Student Loan Data System at the Education Department, a database and tracker of student aid awards. The system includes detailed information on federal student loan borrowers, data that private lenders could potentially use to target students based on their borrowing histories. Such conflict of interest is inherent in the revolving door between the lending industry and its regulatory bodies in government.

Before taking his federal position, Fontana held an executive position at Sallie Mae, the nation's largest for-profit provider of student loans. At least half a dozen other Bush appointments to the Department of Education were also formerly employed at Sallie Mae, including chief operating officer of the Federal Student Aid office Theresa Shaw, Fontana's superior. In 1999, Shaw was senior vice president of Sallie Mae.

Last week, the New York Attorney General's office issued subpoenas to Sallie Mae requesting information on current and former employees who had worked in the Education Department over the past six years.

NINE

Is the US a Good Model for Higher Ed Financing?

Robert Anderson

In the following excerpted viewpoint Robert Anderson examines the politics involved with unversity fees in the United
Kingdom by offering a historical perspective on the British
university system. Students in the United States might find
a particular interest in what the author has to say from a
British and European perspective. Anderson makes thought-
ful points as well about how tuition fees are linked to the
privatization of higher education for profit, and the fact that
British universities are looking to the United States as an
example. An Emeritus Professor of History at the University
of Edinburgh, Anderson has written extensively on the history of universities throughout the British Isles.

Between 1962 and the 1990s higher education in Britain was
effectively free, as the state paid students' tuition fees and
also offered maintenance grants to many. In 1998 university fees
were reintroduced at £1000 per year. In 2004 they were raised to
£3000, now converted into loans repayable on an income-con-
tingent basis, but still regarded as 'top-up' fees supplementing
the state's direct grants to universities. Following the 2010 elec-
tion, the basis of university finance was radically transformed, as
student fees, now raised to £9000, largely replaced the teaching
element in the state grants. This policy applies in England, but
in Scotland free higher education has become a flagship policy

"University Fees in Historical Perspective," by Robert Anderson, History & Policy, February 8, 2016. Reprinted by permission.

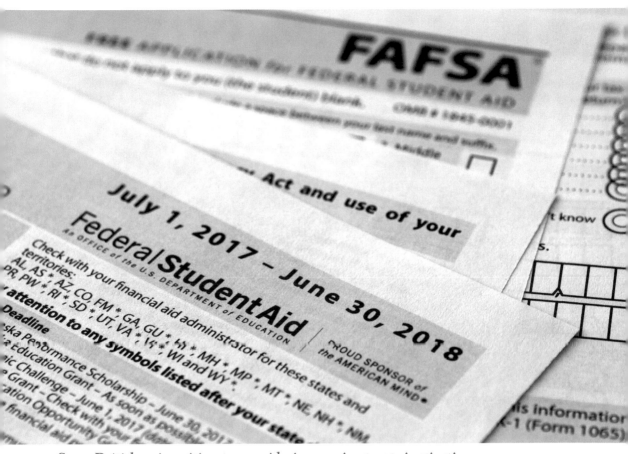

Some British universities are considering moving to a privatization model similar to the United States.

of the Scottish National Party. The Scottish experience, and the collapse in Liberal Democrat support after the party's acceptance of fees as the price of coalition, suggest that free higher education still has electoral appeal, when backed by a firm political will. But in England it seems unlikely that the policy will soon be reversed. Indeed, the Chancellor is abolishing maintenance grants for lower income students from 2016, reducing still further state support for higher education. It is the product of a tide of marketisation which has flowed in one direction since the 1980s, and it is unlikely that any government seeking to mitigate the impact of "austerity" will give priority to abolishing university fees over issues which arouse more passionate popular engagement like the National Health

Service, schools, or welfare. Even in Scotland, the fiscal sustainability of the no-fees policy is questionable, and it has been paid for by cuts elsewhere, including student maintenance grants and further education.

Historical Perspectives

Conservative university policy, as expressed in the White Paper of 2011 (*Students at the heart of the system*) and the Green Paper of 2015 (*Teaching excellence, social mobility and student choice*), is based on clear general principles of choice and competition. But opposition to it often focuses simply on student fees. This is understandable, given their direct impact on students and their families, but fails to address broader issues about how universities are financed and what their relationship with the state should be. Here historians can make a contribution to the debate. History can explain how free higher education came about, and the stages by which it has been eroded. It can put university finance in a longer perspective, reaching back into the 19th century. Historical perspectives are also comparative ones, as national systems have evolved according to their own traditions. There is a broad contrast between continental Europe, where the state has generally controlled and financed universities, and the United States, where they have developed on mixed private and public lines. Britain falls somewhere between. The state played a larger part in university history in the past than is often supposed, and British universities were knitted over the years into a single national system, though one with a clear hierarchy of prestige. This is very relevant to how the marketisation of universities through the fee system may work out in the future.

[...]

There are many practical and ideological arguments both for and against current policies. But a historical perspective underlines their radicalism. They are not a simple development of previous Labour initiatives, or a return to some past utopia of private finance. The current policy in England that fees should cover the whole cost of teaching has no real historical precedent,

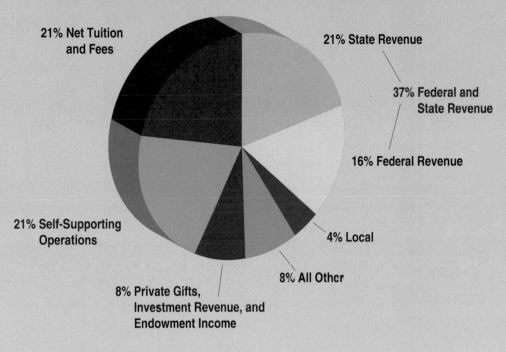

Public higher education institutional revenue for 2013

21% Net Tuition and Fees

21% State Revenue

37% Federal and State Revenue

16% Federal Revenue

21% Self-Supporting Operations

4% Local

8% All Other

8% Private Gifts, Investment Revenue, and Endowment Income

Source: Pew Charitable Trusts

for students have seldom paid the true cost of their education. Moreover, both before 1914 and under the UGC regime until 1989, state funding was only given to universities or colleges which met stringent conditions of quality, under public or charitable governance. Universities were not directly controlled by the state, but nevertheless belonged to the public realm. By decoupling the payment of fees from the subsidy of individual universities, and making them cover the full cost of provision, the field has been made attractive to for-profit organisations. The intention, pushed further in the 2015 Green Paper, is to encourage new "providers" offering cheapness and flexibility. But in the eyes of critics it is part of a wider neoliberal programme of opening public services to globalised corporations, paving the way for general privatisation.

The US Model

English politicians in the Conservative government look for inspiration above all to the United States, rather than to other parts of Europe, or indeed of the United Kingdom. Some European countries retain free higher education, and elsewhere fees are far lower than in England, while Germany has abandoned an experiment with charging fees after popular opposition. The American model itself is more complex than champions of marketisation claim. According to OECD figures, *public* expenditure on higher education in the USA is both a higher proportion of all public expenditure (3.3%) and a higher proportion of GDP (1.4%) than in Britain, where the corresponding figures, below the average for advanced countries, are 2% and 1%. The top-ranking private universities in America are only part of a diverse and flexible system, spread over fifty states, with very unequal standards. While spiralling tuition fees at top universities are making them unaffordable for ordinary middle-class families, the national average is below England's £9,000.

British universities have developed into a single national system, through the addition of successive layers—civic universities, plateglass universities, the technical universities of the 1960s, the new universities of 1992. In the resulting hierarchy, universities were unequal in intellectual and social prestige, but in principle equally accessible. State funding was a guarantor of fairness. But markets in education, left to themselves, will reproduce inequalities of wealth and social capital. This is reinforced by the unique pattern of secondary schooling in England, with its privileged private sector. If the present cap of £9000 is abolished, following the Green Paper proposal that universities which demonstrate "teaching excellence" will be allowed to raise their fees, student choice (illusory anyway when so many universities are highly selective) is likely to lead to new divisions. Teaching reputations, social prestige and research funding already cluster around the 24 universities of the 'Russell Group', whose attraction for students and employers is very apparent in public discussion of university entry and graduate employment. They risk becoming the universities of the rich and socially privileged, leaving second-rank universities for everyone else.

The relation of British universities to the state has a long history; student fees have been part of the mix, but higher education has never previously been abandoned to the market as in England today. Modern states elsewhere support universities because their benefits are social as well as individual, and they have been the creators of individual opportunity, social solidarity, and national identity. The state is unlikely to abandon its interest in them. The combination of core funding and top-up fees introduced by the former Labour government, and adopted in modified form in Wales and Northern Ireland, creates a better balance between student interests, public accountability, academic freedom and democratic access than current entirely unprecedented policies pursued in England which are driven by a market dogma, which should not be allowed to monopolise the debate.

TEN

How the US Government Could End the Student Debt Crisis Today

Raúl Carrillo

In the following viewpoint, Raúl Carrillo compares college students in the United States, who are drowning in debt, with those in Germany, who receive free tuition at all public universities. According to the author, alternatives to higher education, such as government policies to reduce unemployment, are not being promoted by policymakers. Wall Street is profiting from student debt, when the government could make grants to students instead of allowing private companies to profit by managing student loans. Carrillo is an organizer of the Modern Money Network and provides legal support to low-income New Yorkers for the New Economy Project.

Last month, Lower Saxony became the final state in Germany to abolish tuition for all students at public universities. Meanwhile, in the United States, student loan debt has passed the $1 trillion mark. The burden is now becoming increasingly heavy for middle-class and wealthy students, but especially for those from lower-income backgrounds. This injustice has spurred many organizations, like the Occupy Wall Street offshoot Strike

Perhaps most upsetting is the fact that someone is profiting from the student debt crippling our future generations

Debt, to do what they can to pay off student debt on their own.

Borrowers could use the support of their government, but U.S. policymakers don't seem to see student debt through the same moral lens as officials in many other countries do. Can you imagine Secretary of Education Arne Duncan, for example, arguing that "Tuition fees are socially unjust," as German member of Parliament Dorothee Stapelfeldt told *The Times* of London? Or even, as she went on to say, that, "[fees] particularly discourage young people who do not have a traditional academic family background from taking up studies"?

Instead, higher education is peddled as the ticket to economic security by the federal government, commercial lenders, and universities—no matter the cost. Policies that would reduce the fear of unemployment, like the Job Guarantee programs supported by President Franklin Delano Roosevelt and demanded by Martin Luther King Jr., might make it more feasible for young people to opt out of college. Yet policymakers in the United States seem unwilling to consider such options.

Thus, as sociologist Tressie McMillan Cottom has argued, many young Americans, especially people of color, are desperate for higher education. Yet day by day, the student-debt status quo taxes borrowers while doing less and less to subsidize social mobility.

But the worst part is that it doesn't have to be this way. To put it bluntly, there is no fiscal reason why the U.S. student debt crisis should exist.

At a basic level, the U.S. federal government doesn't need to scrimp and save to fully fund higher education. It can just spend money rather than lend it, without incurring any significant negative economic consequences. Although I'd love to reduce spending on, say, prisons, the federal government doesn't even need to take money out of other programs in order to alleviate student debt.

You may find this argument hard to believe. The way most politicians and journalists talk about the national debt and deficit spending makes free higher education sound impossible. But there's another way of looking at the problem, a vision advocated by a growing movement of economists, lawyers, students, and financial practitioners who deal with the institutional nuts and bolts of the economy on a day-to-day basis.

Uncle Sam Can't Go Broke

When progressives advocate for more federal spending on education, the rejoinder is often something like: "OK, but how are you going to pay for it?" Progressives then either fall silent or perform fiscal gymnastics.

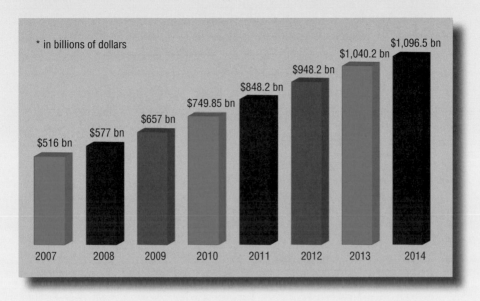

Outstanding federal student loans, 2007-2014*

* in billions of dollars

$516 bn — 2007
$577 bn — 2008
$657 bn — 2009
$749.85 bn — 2010
$848.2 bn — 2011
$948.2 bn — 2012
$1,040.2 bn — 2013
$1,096.5 bn — 2014

Source: US Department of Education, via Huffington Post

But we shouldn't bow to those discussion terms.

First things first: Uncle Sam isn't broke. In fact, the U.S. federal government can't go broke. Up until August 1971, the amount of dollars in the world was pegged to the amount of gold in federal vaults. But it hasn't been that way since we left the gold standard four decades ago. When Congress spends, the Treasury simply asks the Federal Reserve to add or remove money from bank accounts with keystrokes. The dollars don't come from anywhere else. Unlike a business or a household, the federal government spends money into existence.

From this perspective, the U.S. ceased to be capable of "going broke." Many economists known as "deficit owls " have argued for decades that the U.S. federal government doesn't need tax revenues or bond payments in order to spend money on education or anything else. Rather, the true limits to federal spending are the availability of real resources and the stability of prices. Noted hippies like Alan Greenspan, Ben Bernanke, and economists at the St. Louis Federal Reserve have all publicly stated as much.

The fiscal framework of the U.S. government is thus different from that of, say, Detroit—which cannot print its own dollars—or Greece, which now uses euros and can no longer print drachmas. As Warren Buffet stated in 2011, "We've got the right to print our own money. That's the key."

So why do politicians and others keep insisting that the U.S. government can't afford to spend money on education? The notion reflects a confused picture of how our economy actually works.

When people think of federal spending, they often imagine that the government collects money from taxpayers and foreign investors (i.e., China), and then redistributes it for various purposes.

But this picture doesn't reflect how things are really done. The federal government instead spends money into the real economy and drains it via taxes and bonds.

Imagine the economy as a sink full of dishes, with the federal government in control of a tap. In order for us to do the dishes, we need enough water but not so much that our sink overflows. To keep the sink from overflowing, we can open a drain, which removes water from the sink. This is the main macroeconomic function of federal taxes: to drain money from the economy and thus prevent inflation.

Education Spending, Lending, and Inflation

Despite what politicians often say, pumping more money into the economy by running a deficit does not necessarily cause inflation—that is, a general, continuous rise in prices across the economy.

Rather, enduring effects on prices depend upon many factors, including where money goes and what kind of demand it stimulates. Notably, in modern U.S. history, inflation has typically arisen from actions taken by parties other than the U.S. government. For example, inflation during the 1970s can be chiefly attributed to OPEC spiking oil prices, which exacerbated commodity speculation and caused wages and prices to spiral in other sectors. Federal spending was not the culprit.

Inflation can occasionally result from "too much money chasing too few goods." But as any credible economic forecaster will tell you, this is not a salient concern for the U.S. economy right now.

In any case, worries about inflation aren't particularly relevant to a change in funding for higher education. It's important to remember that the government is already pumping new money into the higher education sector; it just does it in the form of loans instead of spending.

Just as importantly, private banks are also creating new "money" every day via student loans, with few people ringing the inflation alarm. As the Bank of England recently detailed, private banks in the modern era do not lend pre-existing funds, but instead create credit "out of thin air" as they lend. When you receive a loan, the bank places funds in your account, simultaneously expanding both the asset and liability sides of its own balance sheet. Again, the dollars don't come from anywhere—they're new.

The point is, if you're not worried about lending causing inflation right now, you shouldn't be worried about robust government spending causing inflation either.

So if there's no economic harm from public funding for higher education, why do young people like 24-year-old Nathan Hornes have college degrees, tens of thousands of dollars in debt, but no full-time job?

As Stephanie Kelton, chair of the economics department at the University of Missouri, Kansas City, recently argued in a seminar on student debt, the problem is "austerity memes" and related myths about inflation. Instead of funding education like a public good, the government is going in the wrong direction, spending almost 10 percent less on total federal aid now than it did in 2010.

Who Should Owe Whom?

If money should be owed for higher education at all, perhaps the federal government should owe us. After all, Article I, Section 8 of the Constitution entrusts the federal government with a monopoly to create, spend, and regulate money for the "general welfare of the United States." And in the era of modern money, there's no good economic reason for students' pockets to be so shallow when the government's are so deep.

When the federal government lists a deficit, that indicates a surplus for American citizens, as well as foreign businesses that sell us goods. In other words, the government's red ink is the public's black ink. Despite what organizations with wholesome and appealing names like Fix the Debt, The Can Kicks Back, and Up To Us, might claim, the "national debt" is not a burden for young people. Indeed, advocating for smaller federal deficits hurts student debtors. Even in the future, it offers them no tangible benefits.

As the Nobel-winning economist Paul Samuelson once acknowledged, the "superstition" that the budget must be balanced at all times is part of an "old fashioned religion," meant to hush people who might otherwise demand the government create more money. Young people should beware of anyone who tells them that their chief worry for the future is the government's debt, rather than their own.

ELEVEN

Should Community College Be Free?

Eric Kelderman and Scott Carlson

> In the following viewpoint, Eric Kelderman and Scott Carlson point out some of the merits of eliminating tuition for all students at certain kinds of post-secondary institutions. What federal and state policies will serve students needs, and how will this affect the for-profit sector? Small private colleges are not merely serving affluent students, but are graduating more low-income students than community colleges or universities are. The authors examine the tricky business of government funding, and how government policies can shape the way the next generation will be educated. Kelderman and Carlson write for the *Chronicle of Higher Education*.

President Obama's proposal to make community college free is getting an enthusiastic reception from two-year colleges and their advocates across the nation. Not surprisingly, though, representatives of other higher-education sectors aren't quite so bullish. One of their greatest fears: that the plan, if enacted, could end up pushing a large number of students away from their institutions and into community colleges.

Here's a look at several groups of institutions with something at stake—and at how they've responded to the proposal.

"Who Has a Stake in Obama's Free Community-College Plan?" by Eric Kelderman and Scott Carlson, *The Chronicle of Higher Education*, January 9, 2015. Reprinted by permission.

For-Profit Colleges

It's hard not to see the president's proposal as a direct shot at proprietary colleges, which have been targets of criticism from the administration for high costs and high loan-default rates. A program that makes public community colleges free could further cut into enrollment, wrote Jeffrey R. Silber, a financial analyst at BMO Capital Markets.

"If these proposals were implemented," according to Mr. Silber, "we believe it would have a negative impact on the for-profit sector, particularly on schools with a high percentage of associate and certificate degrees."

In addition, the plan would designate federal money specifically for community colleges, unlike existing financial-aid funds, which students can access at any participating institution. That could mean a shift in enrollments from for-profits to community colleges, said Claudia Goldin, a professor of economics at Harvard University.

But some reasons that might drive a student to choose a for-profit college over a community college come down to convenience, not cost, said Constance A. Iloh, a higher-education researcher and Ph.D. candidate at the University of Southern California's Pullias Center for Higher Education. "These factors included being able to support family, campus proximity to home and work, flexible class schedules, and the accelerated nature of the program," Ms. Iloh wrote, with her co-author William G. Tierney, in a study published in August by the *Teachers College Record*.

A spokesman for the Association of Private Sector Colleges and Universities, the for-profit sector's main lobbying group, said that the organization would not be issuing a response to the plan.

Private Colleges

News of President Obama's initiative met with skepticism among some private-college presidents, who wonder why community colleges are being singled out as a gateway to higher education.

Small, less-selective private colleges have long struggled against a stereotype that they are expensive and mainly serve

One important thing to consider when choosing a college is its commitment to recruiting and future employment.

affluent students. In fact, they enroll significant numbers of low-income, first-generation, and at-risk students, and they graduate those students at much higher rates than do community colleges. And just like two-year colleges, small four-year colleges have long dealt in preprofessional programs, too.

"I wish the Obama administration would not leave out the small private colleges that actually do the same work that community colleges do," said Patricia McGuire, president of Trinity Washington University.

Some small-college presidents see Mr. Obama's proposal as something that might cannibalize their programs while sacrificing the educational experience. "Once you are into the two-year system, not all two-year colleges are the same, and they're not all good, and students don't always have the ability to discriminate,"

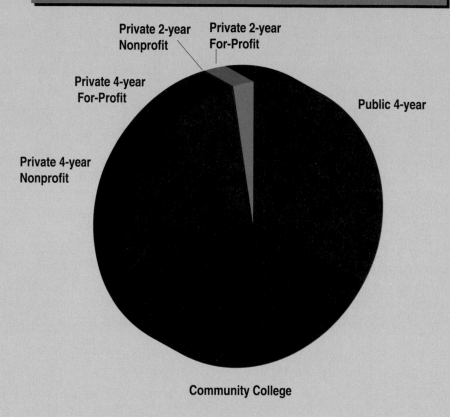

Percentage of US students enrolled by institutional type

Private 2-year Nonprofit

Private 2-year For-Profit

Private 4-year For-Profit

Public 4-year

Private 4-year Nonprofit

Community College

Source: NCES Digest of Education Statistics, 2010–2011

said Ed L. Schrader, president of Brenau University, a Georgia institution that has extensive preprofessional programs.

Experts can't predict if the Obama plan would endanger small, private colleges by undercutting enrollment in the first two years. W. Scott Friedhoff, vice president for enrollment and college relations at the College of Wooster, in Ohio, said that applicants to his institution are not also considering enrolling at a two-year college. But he noted that less-selective private colleges would probably be pinched by the new plan, should it become reality.

Others aren't so sure. "People already choose to go to four-year institutions, whether they are public or private, for reasons other than price," said Sarah A. Flanagan, vice president for government relations and policy development at the National Association of Independent Colleges and Universities. If the plan sends people to college who wouldn't normally enroll—and who may become transfer students at private colleges—"everyone would benefit," she said.

Other Public Colleges

The impact on other public colleges could be quite different, depending on the size and mission of the institution.

Regional comprehensives, where most students in public four-year colleges are enrolled, could be the most heavily affected by the president's proposal. The American Association of State Colleges and Universities, which represents some 400 of those colleges, issued a statement warning of the long-term costs of the plan and the shifting of resources to community colleges at the expense of other sectors.

"A thorough examination must include whether such an allocation of limited federal financial resources focused on eliminating tuition at a subset of institutions for all students is the optimal strategy," the organization said.

Flagship universities—which can, in many cases, recruit students both nationally and internationally—would probably feel less competition for students from community colleges. But like public regional institutions, they are concerned that state and federal money for higher education is already scarce and could become more so if many states participate in the president's plan.

While nearly every higher-education organization is responding to President Obama's plan, the Association of Public and Land-Grant Universities declined through its spokesman to comment on the president's proposal. "We need to learn more about the proposal before commenting," Jeff Lieberson, the group's vice president for public affairs, wrote in an email.

F. King Alexander, president of the Louisiana State University system, said he understood the concerns of the regional institutions.

"If the same concept had included support for four-year institutions, you would have their full support," said Mr. Alexander, a former president of California State University of Long Beach who has spoken out in favor of a proposal to use federal aid as a way to leverage more state money.

That plan, put forth by the American Association of State Colleges and Universities, would establish a "maintenance of effort" requirement, setting "a threshold of state financial support required in order to receive federal funding."

The president's plan could be "very helpful to all of higher education if it ensures that state investment increases down the road," he said.

But it would be a big problem if the federal money simply supplanted state and local dollars, Mr. Alexander said. "States have discovered this trick: Once the federal government puts its money in, they pull their money out."

TWELVE

Free College Tuition Is a Bad Idea

Bob Luebke

> In the following viewpoint, Bob Luebke argues that colleges with no tuition fees will attract students not suited for education. Why give away something that is supposed to have value? Doesn't that cheapen a college education? In addition, Luebke points out, free tuition isn't technically "free," as someone or something has to cover the costs. The author offers suggestions that he feels are better, for example incentivizing corporate educational benefits will be more effective than making college educations approachable to a wider spectrum of students. Luebke is Senior Policy Analyst at the Civitas Institute.

Anyone watching the higher education landscape these days can't help but note the proliferation of articles calling for free tuition. President Obama's January 2015 proposal to make the first two years of community college free spawned much of this discussion. While the proposal stalled, it did help to ignite a nationwide discussion.

Last month, *The Chronicle of Higher Education* ran "*Nobody Should Have to Pay to Go to College*," by Kenneth W. Warren and Samir Sonti. Earlier this month, *The New York Times* ran an opinion piece by Stephanie Saul that advocated free tuition at Harvard to help fuel diversity. Political candidates are also entering the discussion. Democratic presidential candidates Sen. Bernie Sanders

Would higher education have less impact if it were free and available to all?

and former Secretary of State Hillary Clinton have offered proposals for free college and debt-free college respectively.

So what are we to make of these proposals? Advocates claim the United States is simply not educating enough students to maintain our economy and standard of living. These advocates claim college costs and crushing student debt are leading to a shortage of skilled, educated talent, jeopardizing our economic future and making us unable to compete in a global marketplace.

We need to make it easier for students to access a college education—or so the argument goes.

An Educated and Skilled Workforce

If you're a young person, a college student or the parent of a soon-to-be college student, free tuition might sound like a great idea. The prominence of these proposals certainly warrants a closer look.

For starters, we should examine the assumptions underlying this proposal. Some elements of the current discussion defy logic. If something is valuable, shouldn't we be willing to pay for it? So how can we say it has value, yet seek to give it away?

And what about the notion the United States does not have enough educated and skilled people to fill all the positions of the new economy? Some workforce analysts assert that by 2020 two in three jobs will require some higher education to perform. The solution, we're told, is to get more people into school and produce more college graduates.

That makes sense to some, but I'd ask: Is more higher education the only way to get an educated and skilled workforce? Of course, if you're talking about some jobs, that may be the answer. However, we also have labor shortages in fields such as computing, the skilled trades, auto mechanics and health care. Many jobs in these fields pay well, but don't require a four-year degree.

Is there a shortage or merely a maldistribution of students? The sad fact is that for every student in business, engineering or a pre-professional program, there are others in less marketable areas such as art history, psychology and history majors. That's nothing against those fields or those who choose to study in them. But we need to ask: Will our nation be better if we keep generating graduates who have difficulty finding gainful employment?

Is a College Degree Overrated?

Our society values a college degree—maybe too much. Over the last two decades, we've funneled too many young people toward a four-year degree, when the truth is that many probably would have done better elsewhere.

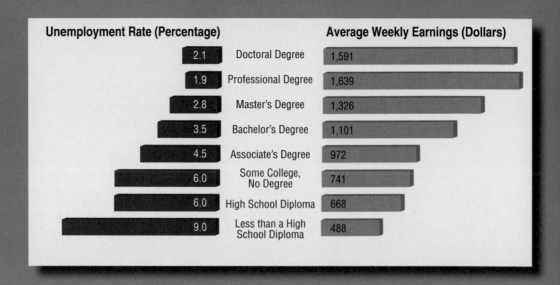

Average weekly earnings and unemployment rates by educational attainment, 2014

Unemployment Rate (Percentage)		Average Weekly Earnings (Dollars)
2.1	Doctoral Degree	1,591
1.9	Professional Degree	1,639
2.8	Master's Degree	1,326
3.5	Bachelor's Degree	1,101
4.5	Associate's Degree	972
6.0	Some College, No Degree	741
6.0	High School Diploma	668
9.0	Less than a High School Diploma	488

Source: U.S. Bureau of Labor

College, unfortunately, has become a proxy for talent. However, the reality is a college education doesn't always translate into social or economic mobility. We tend to overlook the other paths to success, such as starting your own business or becoming an apprentice. We tend to overlook the thousands of individuals who through their own ingenuity, resourcefulness and determination achieved the American dream without ever going to college.

Moreover, newer statistics undercut the idea college is a sure pathway to a good-paying job and prosperity. According to the Economic Policy Institute, wages for university grads are 2.5 percent lower in 2015 than they were in 2000. The research found that the real (inflation-adjusted) hourly wages of recent college grads in 2015 was $17.94 or just over $37,000 a year. In 2000, the average hourly rate was $18.41.[1]

A free tuition proposal would make more sense if there was a great demand for certain fields and college access was a significant problem. But it's not. If you look at the data, the bigger problem is that many students don't finish college. Only about 55 percent of students graduate six years after starting.[2] The problem is not access but completion. Why do people drop out of college? For the most part, money is not the problem. It's usually factors like family issues, or transportation.

Can We Afford Free Tuition?

The Obama program is targeted at community college students, a population where only 21 percent of students earn an associate's degree within three years and only one in five earn an associate's degree and go on to earn a bachelor's degree within six years.

The upshot: Providing free tuition to institutions that graduate a little over 50 percent of their students does not make economic sense. It would likely attract more students that are ill-suited for the college environment who will end up dropping out anyway.

We will likely continue to argue about the value of a college degree. Even if we agree on all questions, any plan to make college tuition free faces significant practical challenges.

Again, let's talk about the president's proposal. The cost of the Obama proposal is approximately $6 billion a year—which seems a bit like a low-ball estimate, but that's another discussion. Seventy-five percent of costs would be borne by the federal government; the states would pay the remainder, about $1.5 billion. You can be sure those costs would only grow. Where states would find the money is a good question.

With a budget deficit of $742 billion and $18 trillion in national debt, Americans should ask: Can we really afford to pay for another program that would in all likelihood quickly become another entitlement? Currently the United States provides billions in student need-based financial aid to eligible low- and middle-income students. The administration's free college proposal would not only reduce the costs of education for many who already qualify for a free or lower-cost education, it would also provide free education for students whose families have the means to pay for part or all of a college education.

In part, working-class families will be forced to subsidize college degrees for rich kids.

Solutions

There is more than one way to position America to be able to compete in a global economy. We must realize many of the problems we seek to redress in higher education are rooted in K-12 education. Substantive school reform and expanding school choice are two proven and less expensive efforts to address these concerns and improve the pool of quality graduates. States might improve this pool by rewarding programs that work. We could also incentivize corporations, such as CVS and UPS, that offer generous higher education benefits to employees of companies.

Unfortunately, the loudest voices in this conversation are advocates for free college tuition. That option can be accomplished in one of two ways. If private institutions, many of which have billion-dollar endowments, chose to provide a tuition-free education, it's their prerogative to spend dollars as they see fit. However, if people want to provide a similar benefit at public universities, the federal government would be the only entity able to administer a free college program.

If we're contemplating that thought, let's remember two things. First, there is no mention of education or higher education in the U.S. Constitution. Unfortunately, that hasn't stopped the federal government from funding and exerting ever more control over K-12 and higher education.

Second, the expansion of federal control across all areas of society has fueled ever-rising costs and resulted in a loss of freedom for institutions and the individual. The track record of federal involvement in education is especially disappointing.

Decades ago, the federal government's interest in universities was limited to research. Then came the GI Bill, student aid and Title IX. The federal government's burgeoning role in research, student aid, diversity, health care and efforts to protect against discrimination has spawned an ever-growing bureaucracy of middle managers. These changes have added tremendously to the cost of higher education, reduced the ability of institutions to respond to changing conditions, and worked to homogenize colleges and universities that were once the envy of the world.

Let's also remember that the one who pays the bill also calls the tune. Colleges and students lose freedom when the federal government intrudes into campus life.

Yes, free college tuition may sound like a dream to some. For most others, it's a nightmare. Let's remember, calling something free doesn't make it free. Nothing in life is free. It's simply a matter of who pays the costs. Free college tuition plans merely shift the costs of education from one group of taxpayers to all taxpayers. The proposals for free college are poorly targeted, too expensive, deliver too little and take away institutional and individual freedoms. It's time to realize free college tuition is too expensive for North Carolina and our nation.

Notes

1. The Class of 2015, Economic Policy Institute, available at: http://www.epi.org/publication/the-class-of-2015/#young-workers-are-not-%E2%80%9Criding-out%E2%80%9D-the-recession-by-%E2%80%9Csheltering-in-school

2. Completing College: A National View of Student Attainment Rates—Fall 2009 Cohort, published by National Student Clearinghouse Research Center, November 2015, Available at: https://nscresearchcenter.org/signaturereport10/

THIRTEEN

Is College Worth the Expense?

Andrew Gillen, Jeffrey Selingo, and Mandy Zatynski

> In the following excerpted viewpoint, Andrew Gillen, Jeffrey Selingo, and Mandy Zatynski call into question the value of a college education in the United States, when weighed against the costs. But measuring the value of a college education isn't simple; there are a number of factors involved. The authors have suggestions for how data on this question could be gathered more effectively. Gillen is a senior researcher at the American Institutes for Research and is on the faculty at Johns Hopkins University. Selingo is an editor for the *Chronicle of Higher Education*. Zatynski is senior editor-writer at The Education Trust.

Most Bang for the Buck

In February, President Barack Obama thrust this return-on-investment question into the national spotlight when he used his State of the Union address to introduce the College Scorecard. This new resource, the president said, would allow parents and students "to compare schools based on a simple criteria: where you can get the most bang for your educational buck." Now there would be a government-backed tool that allowed students to compare colleges the same way consumers size up cars or televisions in *Consumer Reports*.

Gillen, A., Selingo, J., & Zatynski, M. (2013). "Degrees of Value: Evaluating the Return on the College Investment." Washington, DC: American Institutes for Research. Retrieved from http://educationpolicy.air.org/publications/degrees-value-evaluating-return-college-investment. Reprinted by permission.

Is a college education the only way to impress a potential employer?

The idea of applying economic measures to a degree makes most academics uncomfortable. It fails to account for higher education's contributions to society, nor does it measure the less tangible benefits of a college degree, such as improved health, civic engagement, and broad knowledge of the world.

Moreover, not everyone gets the same benefits out of education. "When you come into Staples, you come out with office supplies; when you go into a car dealer, you come out with four wheels and a motor," says Michael Hout, the Natalie Cohen professor of sociology and demography at the University of California at Berkeley. "It's not clear what you come out with, with a college degree. It's a different thing for everybody."

Yet despite its unease with the idea, higher education for decades has been selling its economic returns as the primary reason students and families should pay ever-increasing tuition prices. Indeed, the College Board publishes a report every three years titled *Education Pays*, which presents detailed evidence about the benefits of higher education.

The difference now for higher education is that the data allow comparisons between individual institutions, and by that measure, not all college degrees are created equal. Colleges can no longer simply cite the national averages that they have relied on since the 1970s to sell their degrees at nearly any cost.

In 1974, Jacob Mincer wrote *Schooling, Experience, and Earnings*, a book whose ideas have dominated the discussion about college rates of return ever since. While many had realized that labor market earnings were affected by schooling and work experience, Mincer's key contribution was a clever arrangement that allowed for an easy estimation of what came to be called "the rate of return to education."[1] The Mincer earnings equation has been used to estimate this "rate of return to schooling" ever since, and most analysts find that it is "on the order of 6-10 percent,"[2] meaning that every additional year of schooling tends to increase annual earnings by 6 to 10 percent.

This is a large boost in earnings and, when maintained over decades of paid employment, it means that on average, there will be a large difference between the earnings of college graduates compared with high school graduates. Indeed, some calculations find that over their lifetimes, college graduates earn $1 million more than high school graduates.

[...]

Better Ways to Evaluate ROI

Prestige in higher education is measured not by outputs of how much students learn or by how students fare in the labor market, but mostly by inputs measured by the *U.S. News & World Report* rankings: factors such as faculty salaries, SAT scores, and acceptance rates. As a result of this prestige race, higher education

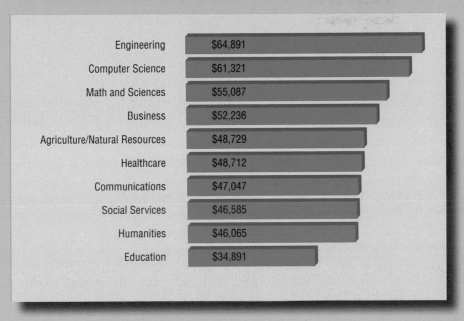

Average salary by undergraduate major for first year after graduation, 2016

Engineering	$64,891
Computer Science	$61,321
Math and Sciences	$55,087
Business	$52,236
Agriculture/Natural Resources	$48,729
Healthcare	$48,712
Communications	$47,047
Social Services	$46,585
Humanities	$46,065
Education	$34,891

Source: National Association of Colleges and Employers

institutions spend an inordinate amount of time, money, and effort investing in those measures that move the rankings, but do not necessarily improve a student's return on investment.

Without adequate measures of institutional outputs, prospective students find themselves lost as they try to differentiate among the colleges they are considering. Their ultimate decisions on where to enroll have real consequences. Consider data produced by College Measures in Virginia. According to this data, graduates of the business program at the University of Richmond earn, on average, $24,000 more a year than those of Virginia State University or Ferrum College. George Mason University business graduates earn about $22,000 more.[3]

That is a significant difference made even more considerable when one looks at the prospect of graduating from any of those institutions with a degree. The six-year graduation rate at Ferrum is 31 percent; at Virginia State, 41 percent; at George Mason, 63 percent; and at Richmond, 87 percent. So not only do some graduates at Virginia State and Ferrum have average first-year salaries that are significantly lower than those of the other two institutions, they are less likely to even make it to graduation day.

Students in every state should have access to this type of information—and more—as they weigh their college decisions. A system to better measure return on investment needs to be national in scope, since a patchwork of state systems will leave many gaps in coverage. Among the factors it should measure:

Graduation and default rates. Both graduation rates and default rates should be expanded to provide more complete and accurate information. Default rates, for example, are reported by cohort, defined as all students who entered repayment within a certain period. However, it would be more useful to distinguish between the default rate of graduates and the default rate of dropouts—and even among graduates with different majors. Similarly, current graduation rates only account for first-time, full-time students, but these students make up less than half of all students currently enrolled in college. Graduation rates should be tracked for all students.

Beyond this, the data to calculate input-adjusted measures should be publicly available. Raw graduation rates make colleges that serve at-risk students look worse than colleges that cater to the affluent. For example, a college that enrolls many low-income students will tend to have a lower graduation rate, even if it provides the same education as a college that enrolls only high-income students. This problem can be avoided by devising input-adjusted graduation rates, which in this example would take into account the income of enrolled students.

Lifetime earnings. First-year earnings matched by College Measures are simply too limiting given that employees' salaries are often volatile in the years right after college graduation. A more useful dataset would show lifetime earnings, sortable by institution and major, and connect to other government data sources, so policymakers could more easily track the earnings of those who received government aid, such as Pell grants or student loans.

Career mapping. When viewed in isolation, career earnings can be misleading, if for example an institution places most of its graduates in public-service fields. A better consumer information system would give students and policymakers a snapshot of the types of jobs graduates from particular colleges and majors end up taking.

Student satisfaction surveys. Satisfaction means a lot, from restaurant outings to doctor visits. If the experience is a good one, that person is likely to recommend it to friends and other peers. College is no exception. By uniformly collecting and reporting results of student satisfaction surveys, prospective candidates would have much richer information about students' experiences in class and on campus, what kind of value they put on their four (or more) years at an institution, and whether they believe the experience helped them land a job.

Higher education has been selling the degree premium for decades as a reason to pay its ever-escalating prices. Now the time has come for colleges and universities to help build a system that gives better information on the value of a college education.

Notes

1. For small values, the difference between natural logged values is approximately equal to the percentage change. By taking the natural log of earnings as the dependent variable, the interpretation of the coefficient for the "years of schooling" variable in a regression can be interpreted as the percent increase in earnings from an additional year of schooling. While it is not an actual rate of return, it was similar enough to be called one in the 1970s, and the terminology has stuck ever since.

2. Daron Acemoglu and Joshua Angrist. "How Large are the Social Returns to Education? Evidence from Compulsory Schooling Laws." NBER Working Paper No. 7444, December 1999. http://www.nber.org/papers/w7444.

3. Virginia only follows graduates who get their first jobs within the state.

FOURTEEN

Student Loans for People with Disabilities Are a Good Investment

Sarah Trick

> In the following viewpoint, Sarah Trick explores the obstacles that students with disabilities face when securing financial aid and loans for college. The author uses her own experience to illustrate how complex the system can be to navigate. Often students aren't able to attend their first choice of universities because of the combined factors of accessibility and aid. When the systems fail to work together, students are at risk of slipping through the cracks. Finding better solutions to this problem is essential, because statistics show that post-secondary education improves employability for people with a disability. Trick is a Canadian journalist who writes on accessibility issues and other topics.

When I first started my undergraduate degree, someone told me not to worry about taking out too many loans, since if I never found a job I wouldn't have to repay them, due to my permanent disability. Making a plan for my future that took as a given living in poverty for a decade seemed unwise. In both Canada, where I live, and the United States, the bar to prove inability to work is extremely high, and doing so may disqualify a person from seeking aid for further education or employment.

"Are Students with Disabilities Served Well by Student Loans?" by Sarah Trick, March 2017. Reprinted by permission.

Students with disabilities face unique challenges when it comes to student aid.

Education Is Essential for Employment

Fortunately, the investment in one's future is likely to pay off. Although the unemployment rate for adults with disabilities is higher than for those without, across all age groups, education ameliorates this effect. In other words, the more educated you are, the more likely you are to participate in the labor force, even with a disability. According to the United States Bureau of Labor Statistics, 48% of adults with disabilities with a Bachelor's degree or higher were employed in 2015, compared to just 24% for those who had finished high school. There are further grants available for adaptive technology and the other educational supports that students with disabilities need, such as attendant care while at school, in recognition of the fact that students with disabilities face a higher financial burden than others when pursuing their goals. In Canada there are grants for specialized equipment and help, which breaks down barriers further.

For the most part, these programs work well and allow many more people to pursue their education. The option to delay repayment especially makes taking student loans a viable prospect, for it often takes us longer to find stable employment. For many, the six-month grace period won't be sufficient time to be able to pay back the loans. However, in my experience and in those shared with me by friends, it is clear that many fall through the cracks, and that the programs cause bureaucratic headaches and heartache for some.

Educational Bureaucracies

My theory about why this is has to do with the nature of educational bureaucracies. Although there exist many Canada-wide programs for students with disabilities, student loan programs are administered by the student's province of origin. In the United States, funding for specialized costs is granted through vocational rehabilitation programs, which vary state-by-state and are subject to different conditions. For example, I spoke with one student who had her funding cut when she changed majors partway through her program of study because the new major was judged

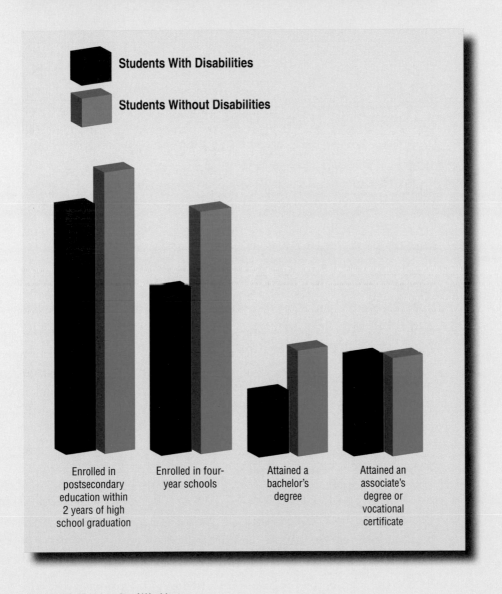

Representation of disabled students in postsecondary education

■ Students With Disabilities

■ Students Without Disabilities

Enrolled in postsecondary education within 2 years of high school graduation

Enrolled in four-year schools

Attained a bachelor's degree

Attained an associate's degree or vocational certificate

Source: DO-IT, University of Washington

less likely to obtain her a job in the future, so it wasn't considered a good investment for the state. These programs also cut students off if they don't achieve certain grade point averages. Funding is available, but it is state-, subject-, and school-specific, and very complex. As well, it is not as easy to access this funding if a student is unable to take a full courseload, which many students with disabilities are not. In the United States, federal Pell Grants are only available to full-time students (though some schools kick in additional funding.) In Canada, a student can still have funding with a reduced courseload, but only to a certain amount—part-time loan finding is governed by different rules and does not include eligibility for as many grants.

In Canada, student assistance is administered by the provinces. I went to school out of province for accessibility purposes. Although I qualified for financial aid, it needed to be administered through my home province. This meant there were many scholarships and bursaries from which I was barred from applying, including ones specifically for students with disabilities, because their application criteria was eligibility for provincial student loans, not eligibility for financial assistance in general. This meant that there was equipment and other costs that could not be covered.

When mental health issues are in play, things become even more difficult. When students need to withdraw, even temporarily, from school due to mental health reasons, or if they fail courses, they are often required to pay back their loans and deal with exhausting appeals. When the waters are muddied by failing grades, as can happen when mental health issues become severe, sometimes people become ineligible for further terms of study. They also lose access to the low-cost treatment offered at most universities, which can leave them further behind than when they started and with less chance of becoming well enough to resume their studies, leaving them stuck in a catch-22.

On the whole, the programs designed for students with disabilities are well-thought-out, and the exclusion criteria make sense. What I would like to see going forward is more of these programs talking to each other, to ensure fewer students in exceptional or unusual circumstances fall through the cracks, and everyone can access the financial aid that would make the most sense for them, instead of trying to make it so no one can possibly get anything "extra" or "more than they deserve." Most of all, I would like to see more support of post-secondary students graduating and moving into the workforce, so that these loans and grants are a prudent investment for everyone involved. Although it is good to see that a college degree makes people with disabilities more likely to be employed, the Bureau of Labor Statistics also says labor force participation is around 50 percentage points lower for those with disabilities than without, when compared with others of similar age and educational attainment. Like every other student, students with disabilities take out loans as an investment in their futures. The best thing to do for them is make sure those futures are possible.

What You Should Know About Student Loans

What to Think About When Considering Student Loans

- Apply for government grants as well as student loans

- In both the US and in Canada, one form is used for both grants and loans

- Apply for student loans and financial aid through your state government

- The National Association of State Financial Aid Administrators keeps an online directory of programs offered to residents in every state. Check this directory even if you plan to attend school in another state! Many states have tuition exchange programs with other states or in a region.

- In the US, apply through Free Application for Federal Student Aid https://fafsa.ed.gov

- Also apply for Federal Work-Study Program https://www2.ed.gov/programs/fws/index.html

- In Canada, apply for grants and loans through Canada Student Loans https://www.canada.ca/en/employment-social-development/services/student-financial-aid/student-loan/student-loans.html and work-study programs on campus.

- Students who qualify for a grant and a loan may accept them and give back the loan right away

- Apply for private grants, scholarships, and bursaries as well as government ones

- Ideally you will meet your school costs without a loan, or only a small loan during your last semester

- If you are employed, ask about financial aid benefits. Many businesses will provide funds for employees, some for children of employees. Read the company's website, ask your union.

- Ask professional associations or unions representing people in the career you want to enter; they will have advice about what training to get, what co-op work study is available. They might have bursaries, scholarships, grants, or fellowships. They might have mentor programs to pair students with experienced people.

- Discuss education choices, employment plans, and the cost of school with your family and friends. Your parents might have a savings plan. Your relatives might have support programs from their employer or union. Your relatives and older friends might arrange a job for you in summer or part-time. Your parents might qualify for a PLUS loan to help you (in the US). You or your (Canadian) parents would qualify for a reduction of taxable income. You might be able to live at your parents' home or with a relative for low rent or no rent.

What to Avoid

- Do NOT fall for a scam, high-cost loans or expensive private schools that are not accredited

- Do NOT miss a payment!. The interest rate will often increase if you miss a payment. For the Public Service Loan Forgiveness program, you must never miss a payment. Find out when you have to make payments, and keep track. Payments for most loans start after finishing your studies.

- Stafford loans that are not subsidized need interest payments starting right away. Set up payments with your bank. If you're still in school, or going back, you might not be charged interest—find out. Part-time studies might mean you don't have to make payments yet—find out.

- Do NOT take on loans at high interest rates with payments you can't expect to make

- Do NOT take on credit card debt. Pay any credit card purchases immediately or don't use cards.

- Do NOT spend grants or loans on anything but basic school costs. No booze or partying!

- Do NOT spend money after graduation on anything but basic work costs and paying debt.

What You Should Do About Student Loans

Today, the process of applying for financial aid and student loans can be confusing and complicated. It's important to not get discouraged and to make good use of all the funding opportunities available to you

Start by writing out your plans and options. Student financial aid takes many forms, including grants and loans from federal and state (or provincial) governments; bursaries, scholarships, awards from governments, unions, businesses, social groups; on-campus employment; fellowships; co-op degrees with work/study employment in an industry related to your major; research assistants and teaching assistants; and student association participation.

Meet with advisors about student financial aid. You can take advantage of advisors at your school; at the college or university where you plan to enroll; at other colleges or universities in your area to know your alternatives; and by e-mail and phone.

Make note of student financial aid for which you might qualify. Think about all the different aspects of your life and your family. Make a long list and consider programs while in the military, reserves or cadets, programs for after military service; military family member programs, veterans associations; programs for people with a disability: grants, loans, tutoring, accessibility assistance; programs through your parents' employers; programs through local charities and nonprofit associations (Rotary, Rebekahs, Legions etc); language or culture-based programs; options for mature students.

Keep track of your expected expenses. To reduce your expenses, consider searching for used books through campus bookstores and online sites. You might qualify for subsidized transit bus passes, which are cheaper than a car. To avoid high-priced housing, share accommodations or live with family. Use campus and library computers and free Wi-Fi.

You also should make note of all the expectations for any loan you accept. Consider the repayment expectations and what happens if you default. How would you qualify for interest deferral and repayment assistance programs? Ask whether loan consolidation of some federal loans will lower your interest rates. Many private loans don't allow for loan consolidation. Remember: Bankruptcy is not an option when student loans are a person's only debt.

Calculate how much you will owe; what your monthly payments will be; how long it will take to pay off the debt; what you can do to stop interest accruing; what reasons will allow part or all of the debt to be forgiven; how employment in federal service or military will affect the debt; what happens if you have a disability or a profound permanent health change.

Consider education alternatives that might serve you well, such as community adult education. Community college can provide valuable training for employment, as can apprenticeship programs in the trades for a year or two before transferring to a four-year college. Compare the cost of private for-profit post-secondary education facilities with state universities and community colleges. Is the higher tuition worth it? Will specialization and jobs make up for debt load?

Ask yourself "Does college cost more for me—or bring more to me—than it might others?" Consider the benefit of taking out student loans instead of the alternatives. For instance, part-time employment can have negative effects on grades and can extend the length of time it takes to complete your degree. Credit card debt or lines of credit have higher rates of interest than student loans. Also consider the pros and cons of support or funding from family or friends. For instance, your parents receive a tax deduction for tuition fees so the net expense is reduced. Consider also options to choose employment and part-time or minimal studies, rather than full-time studies.

The business of student loans is much more complicated than most teenagers are accustomed to. Having honest, frank discussions with your family and using all available resources can help ensure that you plan for your future without being saddled with a lifelong debt.

ORGANIZATIONS TO CONTACT

The editors have compiled the following list of organizations concerned with the issues debated in this book. The descriptions are derived from materials provided by the organizations. All have publications or information available for interested readers. The list was compiled on the date of publication of the present volume; the information provided here may change. Be aware that many organizations take several weeks or longer to respond to inquiries, so allow as much time as possible.

Canada Student Loans
National Student Loans Service Centre
PO Box 4030
Mississauga, ON L5A 4M4
Canada
website: www.canada.ca/en/employment-social-development/services/student-financial-aid/student-loan/student-loans.html

In Canada, students can apply for both grants and loans through Canada Student Loans. The website has links also to provincial financial aid programs for students.

Consumer Financial Protection Bureau
PO Box 2900
Clinton, IA 52733-2900
(855) 411-2372
website: www.consumerfinance.gov

This government agency operates to inform citizens and to make sure that banks, lenders, and other financial companies treat people fairly. The consumer tools and educational resources are useful for all kinds of debt including student loans.

Federal Student Aid—US Department of Education
(800) 433-3243

website: https://studentaid.ed.gov

At this website, information is available about getting money for higher education, from the government and other sources: grants, scholarships, loans, work-study programs, and aid for military families. There is also advice on avoiding scams. This site has many resources from college preparation to repayment information, including deferment and forgiveness and discharge.

Federal Student Loan Support Center
(800) 557-7394

website: https://studentloans.gov

This page has resource links, an email contact form, and a form for a live web chat with an agent. Open seven days a week except federal holidays.

FedLoan Servicing
PO Box 69184

Harrisburg, PA 17106-9184

(855) 265-4038

website: https://myfedloan.org

FedLoan Servicing was established to support the US Department of Education's ability to service student loans owned by the federal government. It is one of a limited number of organizations approved by the Department of Education to service loans owned by the federal government. The organization provides dedicated loan counselors.

National Association of State Financial Aid Administrators (NASFAA)

1801 Pennsylvania Avenue NW, Suite 850
Washington, DC 20006-3606
(202) 785-0453
website: www.nasfaa.org

NASFAA keeps an online directory of financial aid programs in every state. Programs are offered to residents, but many states have exchange programs with other states.

Scholarships.com

website: www.scholarships.com

This website has an international database for scholarships and a college search for detailed information on over four thousand colleges and universities.

Scholarships Canada

website: www.scholarshipscanada.com

This website has information on scholarships available for students in Canada.

US Department of Education

400 Maryland Avenue SW
Washington, DC 20202
(800) 872-5327
website: www.ed.gov

The US Department of Education is a government agency whose mission is to promote student achievement and preparation for global competitiveness by fostering educational excellence and ensuring equal access.

BIBLIOGRAPHY

Books

Beth Akers and Matthew M. Chingos, *Game of Loans: The Rhetoric and Reality of Student Debt*. Princeton, NJ: Princeton University Press, 2016. Makes the case that college is still a good investment for most students and addresses what the authors say are the real problems facing student lending.

Sandy Baum, *Student Debt: Rhetoric and Realities of Higher Education*. New York, NY: Palgrave Macmillan, 2016. Tells the true story of student debt in America with careful analysis and policy recommendations for bringing down student debt.

Committee on Finance United States Senate, *Less Student Debt from the Start: What Role Should the Tax System Play?* CreateSpace, 2015. Transcript of the US Senate's 2014 hearing on tax reform, specifically the role it plays on student loans and college education and how the US government can make student loans more manageable.

William Elliott and Melinda Lewis, *Student Debt: A Reference Handbook* (Contemporary World Issues). Santa Barbara, CA: ABC-CLIO, 2017. Considers whether the cost of higher education is simply too high, explains what is contributing to the rising rate of borrowers defaulting on their loans, and predicts whether the student loan bubble is about to pop.

Reyna Gobel, *Graduation Debt: How to Manage Student Loans and Live Your Life*, 2nd edition. Boston, MA: Houghton Mifflin Harcourt, 2014. Provides tangible tips and a road map for managing student loan debt and maintaining healthy finances throughout life.

Sara Goldrick-Rab, *Paying the Price: College Costs, Financial Aid, and the Betrayal of the American Dream*. Chicago, IL: University of Chicago Press, 2016. Drawing on a groundbreaking study, examines why America is in a student debt crisis and offers solutions to fixing the problem.

Cryn Johannsen, *Solving the Student Loan Crisis: Dreams, Diplomas & A Lifetime of Debt.* Los Angeles, CA: New Insights Press, 2016. Addresses the student loan crisis and the families who struggle from it while what has become a higher education machine profits.

Andrew P. Kelly and Sara Goldrick-Rab, *Reinventing Financial Aid: Charting a New Course to College Affordability.* Cambridge, MA: Harvard Education Press, 2016. Two experts debate the growing problem of student lending, to serve as a counterpoint to the consensus that got us in the trouble we're in.

Adam S. Minsky, *Student Loan Debt 101.* CreateSpace, 2015. Written by a student loan attorney, this is a practical guide for managing student debt.

Carla Mooney, *Teen Guide to Paying for College.* San Diego, CA: Reference Point Press, 2017. Teaches teens how to navigate the college funding maze, using grants, scholarships, loans, and other creative options to pay for school.

GS Prentzas, *Smart Strategies for Paying for College.* New York, NY: Rosen Publishing, 2015. Helps students accurately assess their financial situations and develop strategies to finance a college education.

Periodicals

Richard Adams and Sonia Sodha, "Tuition Fees Should Be Scrapped, Says 'Architect' of Fees Andrew Adonis," *Guardian*, July 7, 2017. https://www.theguardian.com/education/2017/jul/07/tuition-fees-should-be-scrapped-says-architect-of-fees-andrew-adonis.

Jillian Berman, "How Student Loans Make Successful People Feel Like Frauds." MarketWatch, June 28, 2017. http://www.marketwatch.com/story/how-student-loans-make-successful-people-feel-like-frauds-2017-06-28.

Pamela Brown, "The Metastasis of Economic Hate." *South Atlantic Quarterly*, 203 Volume 112, #4, pp. 804–911. saq.dukejournals.org/content/112/4/804.abstract.

Cole135G, "I'm the Brother of the Student Who Committed Suicide Yesterday Morning." UWaterloo Thread. Reddit.com, March 21, 2017. https://www.reddit.com/r/uwaterloo/comments/60qoni/im_the_brother_of_the_student_who_committed/.

Stacy Cowley and Jessica Silver-Greenberg, "As Paperwork Goes Missing, Private Student Loan Debts May Be Wiped Away." *New York Times*, July 17, 2017. https://www.nytimes.com/2017/07/17/business/dealbook/student-loan-debt-collection.html?smid=fb-nytimes&smtyp=cur.

M. Gleeson, "Student Loan Debt and the Effects on the Broader Economy." *Johns Hopkins University*, April, 2016. https://jscholarship.library.jhu.edu/bitstream/handle/1774.2/.../Michael%20Gleeson.pd.

Ryan Gorman, "How Student-Loan Debt Is Dragging Down the Economy," *Business Insider*, May 1, 2015. http://www.businessinsider.com/3-charts-explain-the-effect-of-student-loans-on-the-economy-2015-5.

Abigail Hess, "This Epic Clerical Error Could Wipe Out $5 billion in Student Loan Debt," CNBC, July 19, 2017. http://www.cnbc.com/2017/07/19/this-clerical-error-could-wipe-out-5-billion-in-student-loan-debt.html.

Kelley Holland. "The High Economic and Social Costs of Student LoanDebt," CNBC, June 15, 2015. http://www.cnbc.com/2015/06/15/the-high-economic-and-social-costs-of-student-loan-debt.html.

May Luong. "The Financial Impact of Student Loans," Statistics Canada, archived 2010. http://www.statcan.gc.ca/pub/75-001-x/2010101/article/11073-eng.htm.

Andy Josuweit. "Want to Join 150,000+ Borrowers in Conquering Student Debt?" Student Loan Hero. https://studentloanhero.com/start-here/.

Anya Kamenetz. "A New Look at the Lasting Consequences of Student Debt," NPREd, April 4, 2017. http://www.npr.org/sections/ed/2017/04/04/522456671/a-new-look-at-the-lasting-consequences-of-student-debt.

Anya Kamenetz. "Teachers, Lawyers and Others Worry About the Fate of Student Debt Forgiveness," NPREd, April 5, 2017. http://www.npr.org/sections/ed/2017/04/05/522575533/teachers-lawyers-and-others-worry-about-the-fate-of-student-debt-forgiveness.

Elyssa Kirkham. "6 Ways Your Student Debt Ultimately Hurts (and Helps) the Economy." Student Loan Hero, December 8, 2016. https://studentloanhero.com/featured/effects-of-student-loan-debt-us-economy//

Alexandra Lanza. "Study: Student Loan Borrowers Delaying Other Life Decisions." US News, January 20, 2016. https://www.usnews.com/education/blogs/student-loan-ranger/articles/2016-01-20/study-student-loan-borrowers-delaying-other-life-decisions.

Katie Lobosco. "New York Just OK'd Free College for Middle Class," CNN, April 10, 2017. http://money.cnn.com/2017/04/08/pf/college/new-york-free-tuition/index.html.

Christopher Newfield. "Let's Undo the Great Mistake—Make University Tuition Free," *Guardian*, July 14, 2017. https://www.theguardian.com/higher-education-network/2017/jul/14/lets-undo-the-great-mistake-make-university-tuition-free?CMP=share_btn_tw.

Katie Rose Guest Pryal. "Collegiality and Disability," *Chronicle Vitae*, February 7, 2017. https://chroniclevitae.com/news/1695-collegiality-and-disability?cid=at&utm_source=at&utm_medium=en&elqTrackId=86828a9954b34ddc86bdf4307a62f-10d&elq=07b6fa77d20440fe9ed407fcf0677333&elqaid=12483&elqat=1&elqCampaignId=5087#sthash.EcmasuWF.skTzCjD0.dpuf.

Anna Sale, "Our Student Loan Secrets," *Death, Sex & Money* podcast, WNYC studios. https://project.wnyc.org/death-sex-money-podcast-student-loans/.

Acacia Squires. "Confused About Your Student Loans? You're Not Alone," *Higher Ed,* NPR.org, February 7, 2016. http://www.npr.org/sections/ed/2016/02/07/465556666/confused-about-your-student-loans-youre-not-alone.

Lam Thuy Vo, "What America Owes in Student Loans," *Planet Money*, NPR.org. April 23, 2012. http://www.npr.org/sections/money/2012/04/18/150909686/what-america-owes-in-student-loans.

Websites

Ask Doctor Debt
(http://www.askdoctordebt.org)

This is a useful resource website run by an association of collection agencies, which answers frequently asked questions and provides a glossary and legal information. These resources and links are useful for other forms of debt as well as student loans and helpful for military families.

NPR: Student Loan Debt
(http://www.npr.org/tags/141862965/student-loan-debt)

Stories on National Public Radio tagged "student loan debt" are collected here. Check also the tags "your money and your life" "education" and "npr ed."

Student Loan Hero
(https://studentloanhero.com)

This website offers articles and information on student loans and makes a particular focus on refinancing, lower payments, income-driven plans, military families, and forgiveness. A useful resource both while in school and later when repaying student debt. Take this advice to heart.

INDEX